FOR YOUR INFORMATION 4

ADVANCED READING SKILLS

Karen Blanchard ◆ Christine Root

Longman

For Your Information 4

Addison Wesley Longman, 10 Bank Street, White Plains, NY 10606

Editorial director: Allen Ascher

Executive editor: Louisa Hellegers

Development editor: Margaret Grant

Director of design and production: Rhea Banker

Managing editor: Linda Moser

Production manager: Alana Zdinak

Production editor: Noël Vreeland Carter

Electronic production supervisor: Kim Teixeira

Senior manufacturing manager: Patrice Fraccio

Photo research: Matthew McConnochie, Diana Nott

Text design: Taurins Design Associates

Cover design: Taurins Design Associates

Text art: Ron Chironna, Dusan Petricic, Steven Greydanus

Photo credits: page 3, Andy Levin/Photo Researchers, Inc.; page 24, © Rubén Guzmán; page 38, Photo "Icebreaker Kapitan Khlebnikov near Balleny Islands," © Jeff Rubin; page 46, © Andy Deering/OmniPhoto Communications, Inc.; page 53, Corbis Digital Stock; page 62, Map © July 13, 1998 *U.S. and World Report*; page 69 © 1995 Anthony Edgeworth; page 77, © 1997 Abigail Seymour; page 83, Library of Congress; page 103, Stephen Green/*Sports Illustrated*; page 110, © 1996 Alan Matheson; page 118, Steven E. Sutton/Duomo Photography Inc.; page 142, Steve Mason/PhotoDisc, Inc.; page 164, Anthony Savignano/Ipol Inc.; page 173, CBS Television; page 183, © The Jim Henson Company; page 197, Photo of Jeff Bezos © Paul Souders/Gamma Liaison; pages 207, 210, 211, 217, 218, Graphs © Time Inc. Reprinted by permission; page 241, John A. Rizzo/PhotoDisc, Inc.

Text credits: See page 266

Library of Congress Cataloging-in-Publication Data
Blanchard, Karen Lourie,
    For your information 4: advanced reading skills / Karen Blanchard, Christine Root.
      p. cm.
    ISBN 0-201-34053-4
    1. English language—textbooks for foreign speakers. 2. Readers.
I. Root, Christine Baker,   II. Title. III. Title: For your information 4.
PE1128.B5862 1999
428.6'4—dc21   99-20124
                                      CIP

3 4 5 6 7 8 9 10-CRS-04 03 02

CONTENTS

For Your Information 4 is a challenging book of authentic readings for low-advanced students of English as a Second Language. It is a reading skill-builder designed for students who have experience with reading from mainstream sources and who are ready to delve into longer and/or more densely written material with nuanced language. *FYI 4* moves away from intensive textual analysis and toward the broader application of reading for the purpose of writing, discussion, and making presentations in academic, professional, or personal settings. It thereby bridges the gap between reading for a controlled ESL setting and independent reading for school, work, or pleasure. It is meant for use in adult education programs, colleges and universities, language institutes, and secondary schools—both in the United States and abroad.

Like *FYI 1, 2,* and *3, FYI 4* is made up of eight thematically based units, each of which contains a selection of articles, interviews, stories, poems, or essays in a wide variety of writing styles. Some selections are rather lengthy. The book is designed to help students engage in the process of reading critically and encourages them to move beyond passive reading to a more active, sophisticated analysis of the material. To this end, students are asked to integrate, discuss, and write about new ideas, as well as to draw on their own knowledge and experience of the topics during in-depth follow-up activities.

The basic format for each unit in *FYI 4* is as follows:

- **Points to Ponder**
  Thought-provoking prereading questions introduce the general topic of each unit and generate discussion and interest.

- **Reading Selections and Tasks**
  Each unit contains two to four authentic reading selections on high-interest topics of universal appeal. Selections are followed by a combination of writing/discussion questions and activities to help students:
    - expand their vocabulary by using context to figure out meaning and define terms and by studying and using word forms;
    - hone their reading skills through a variety of strategies such as previewing, predicting, skimming, scanning, recognizing main ideas, analyzing style and tone, separating fact from opinion, understanding point of view and figurative language, and increasing reading speed;
    - gain experience with exercises that replicate those on the TOEFL®;
    - develop their writing skills by summarizing, paraphrasing, writing reports and essays, and using appropriate quoting and citing conventions

- **Tying It All Together**
  Each unit concludes with a set of questions that encourage students to think about, distill, and discuss the ideas they have read about. Following the questions are a "Just for Fun" activity and a "Reader's Journal" in which students are asked to reflect, in writing, on the ideas and information in each unit.

We hope that you and your students enjoy working through the readings and activities in this text and that you find the text interesting *for your information*.

KLB, CBR

ACKNOWLEDGMENTS

Thank you to Diane Englund and Stephanie Fins for their interest in this project and their unrelenting tenacity in tracking down articles for us. Thanks also to Robby Steinberg for her generosity of time and spirit and for her good judgment. As always, we would like to thank our families, friends, students, and colleagues for their unfailing support.

We dedicate this book to our students, past and present, who have so enriched our lives.

LANGUAGE AND LIFE

FYI

Unit·1

Selections

Times change and so do languages, lives, and for some of us, even our names. As you work your way through the readings in this unit, you will read about the many ways that languages, lives, and names change as time goes by.

POINTS TO
PONDER

DISCUSSION

Think about and then discuss the following questions.

1. When did you decide to make a commitment to learn English at the advanced level? Why did you make this decision?

2. In what ways has it been easy for you? Difficult?

3. Do you anglicize your name when you are with English speakers?

One of the most difficult things about moving to another country is learning a new language. But a new language is only one of the many adjustments new-comers have to make in overcoming culture shock. "What Would You Like in Your Welcome Package?" explores the possibility of compiling a "welcome pack-age" containing helpful information for foreigners living in the United States.

BEFORE YOU
READ

PREREADING
DISCUSSION

1. Have you ever lived in another country? If so, what were the hardest things for you to adjust to?

2. Does your country have a lot of immigrants? What kinds of problems do you think they have adjusting to life in your country?

● ●

SELECTION I

What Would You Like in Your Welcome Package?

Immigrants Offer Tips for an Official Guide to America

BY DAVID W. CHEN

1   If Independence Day celebrates America—fireworks, parades and cascades of red, white and blue—then it also celebrates what it means to be an American. And being an American usually means being an immigrant or a descendant of immigrants.

2   In New York City, this has never been truer: A new wave of arrivals has propelled the city's immigrant population to a record 2.7 million, and about 60 percent of New Yorkers are either immigrants or their children.

3   Many things have changed since the New York area's last huge wave of immigration early in the [twentieth] century. Immigrants take jetliners to Kennedy and Newark International Airports, not ships to Ellis Island. But as any immigrant can attest, the first steps to life in the United States are no less awkward, difficult and lonely.

4   Last year, the United States Commission on Immigration Reform, a Federal advisory body, suggested several ways to help immigrants adjust. One idea was to compile a "welcome package" containing important information in several languages.

5   For now, that suggestion is not being actively considered by the

Immigration and Naturalization Service, which is more concerned with reducing the unprecedented backlog of two million immigrants awaiting citizenship around the country, said Eric Andrus, an I.N.S. spokesman in Washington.

6   The backlog is so great—300,000 are waiting in New York City alone—that the New York immigration district did not have enough approved applications to stage its traditional Fourth of July swearing-in ceremony this year.

7   Given the agency's priorities, it remains to be seen whether the welcome package will ever become a reality.

8   But what if there were such a package? What would be in it? Practical things, like maps or guides to English-language classes? Philosophical things, like strategies for successful immigrant living? Or quirky things to reduce the chances of culture shock?

9   In the spirit of Independence Day, eight immigrants were asked for their thoughts. Some had specific ideas for an official Federal information packet, while others couldn't resist tossing in more personal advice.

10   Sonia Urban, 40, a pastry chef at Maya Restaurant in Manhattan who emigrated in 1970 from the Dominican Republic, suggested including information about the government, about language schools, about the libraries.

11   "In some countries, people don't even know what taxes are," she said. "I would explain the concept, say that it's not money that you give away to the Government; it produces money to support the schools and Medicaid and the libraries."

12   A list of discount outlets and wholesale companies would also be beneficial, she said, as would a guide to the city's culinary delights.

13   "Maybe something visual, like a poster, showing different foods, like french fries," she said. "If you understand what it is, and what it looks like, I think you'll be willing to try it."

14   Liam Benson, who is in his early 50's, owns two bars, O'Donoghue's and The Quiet Woman, in Hoboken, N.J. He was a dairy farmer in County Mayo, Ireland, before immigrating here 15 years ago.

15   Mr. Benson said he would encourage immigrants to avoid living in an area with a large concentration of their own nationality. Being independent, he said, would open one's mind. A positive attitude also helps.

16   "A lot of Irish say that they'll stay one or two years," he said. "Then one year goes by, and they say another year. Then another. Until 10 years go by so fast, and they're still here and they don't achieve their maximum while they're here."

17   People also should not cling to their old habits, he said. For example, immigrants should not gripe about how Americans write dates numerically: 7/4/98, for instance, is written 4/7/98 in Ireland and many other countries. "You're not going to change the American way," Mr. Benson said, "so you might as well go along with it."

18   Florence Moise-Stone, 43, a lawyer for the City University of New York, emigrated from Haiti about 30 years ago. She said that Haitian immigrants would appreciate guides to the city's parks, churches, libraries and ethnic enclaves.

19   One thing that Haitians would have to adjust to, she said, is freedom of speech: "You can go out and bad-mouth Clinton all you want; nothing is going to happen to you."

20   Dame Babou, 45, who emigrated from Senegal 10 years ago and now

works as a radio and newspaper correspondent in Manhattan, said that any package should include tips on where, and how, to master English: "I've observed people who ordered the same type of food for six months, nine months, simply because they didn't know the word for the other foods."

21 He said that Senegalese immigrants should listen primarily to the authorities for advice, and not fellow immigrants.

22 "When I came here, many people said the bank wouldn't accept my money because I didn't have a green card," he said. They were mistaken. "That was only because they happened to have a green card when they opened their bank account."

23 The pace of life here is fast, he warned, and the living spaces mercilessly tiny. Don't take it personally, Mr. Babou said. "People don't have time to give to you, so don't be angry with them."

24 Alfred Baumeler, 32, who emigrated from Peru as a child and grew up in a largely Peruvian immigrant neighborhood in Passaic, N.J., is now a senior brand manager with a pharmaceuticals company in New Jersey. He said that he would enclose a fair amount of information about the selling points of America.

25 "A lot of them are fighting that emotional attachment to their country," Mr. Baumeler said, "so you need to say, 'Here are some of the privileges that come with being a naturalized citizen.'"

26 Complicating that switch, perhaps, is that Peruvians are generally quite sociable, he said, while Americans are more private.

27 "Some Peruvian immigrants construe that as being unfriendly, or find that insulting, or the American people are

cold," he said. "They should realize that people here just keep to themselves."

28 Julie Horvath-Krol, an actress and translator, emigrated from Hungary in 1991. Now a Staten Island resident, she declined to give her age, but cheerily stated that she has six children; the oldest is 29.

29 Topping Ms. Horvath-Krol's list in a fantasy package for immigrants was advice on learning the language and getting familiar with the city's vast library system.

30 In addition, she said, Hungarians should not be afraid of the police. And they should also understand how easy it is to get things done, she said. In Hungary, people just wait and wait in line, sometimes for hours, sometimes for consecutive days. Here, she said, "you can just make an appointment."

31 One thing she wished someone had given her when she first came here was a user-friendly guide to building one's credit history and financial profile.

32 "Teach them that 'yes, there is a way to open a bank account,' which is mutually beneficial for the businesses here and for people coming here," she said.

33 Paul Mak, 40, the president of the Brooklyn Chinese-American Association, came here in 1970 from Hong Kong.

34 He said an immigration packet should include a guide to New York landmarks, a subway map, a map of downtown Manhattan listing major city agencies and a list of city services and telephone numbers that people can call for immediate help.

35 "It can be just as simple as who to call when you want to do construction on your house," he said.

36 Mona Sharma Sachar, 35, founder and associate publisher of *Silicon India*, a business and technology magazine based in Manhattan, emigrated from India in 1985.

37   Ms. Sachar said that the package should include information like contact numbers for consulates, and information on city services like subsidized housing and tax tips.

38   And, she said, it should tell Indian immigrants to change their concept of time: in India, 9 A.M. means 10 A.M. . . . or so. "Here," she said, "a deadline is a deadline."

● ●

A. Read the following statements. If according to the article a statement is true, write *T* on the line. If it is false, write *F*.

_____ 1. Over half of the residents of New York City are either immigrants or children of immigrants.

_____ 2. Today immigrants have an easier time adjusting to the first steps of life in the United States than they did earlier in the twentieth century.

_____ 3. Several million immigrants are waiting to become American citizens.

_____ 4. A welcome package for immigrants is being prepared by the Immigration and Naturalization Service.

_____ 5. In the past immigrants came to the United States by ship; now many come by plane.

B. Match the names and identities.

NAMES	IDENTITIES
_____ 1. Sonia Urban	a. dairy farmer in Ireland who immigrated 15 years ago and now owns two bars
_____ 2. Liam Benson	b. emigrated from Senegal 10 years ago, works as a radio and newspaper correspondent in Manhattan
_____ 3. Florence Moise-Stone	c. actress and translator, emigrated from Hungary in 1991
_____ 4. Dame Babou	d. founder and associate publisher of *Silicon India*, emigrated from India in 1985
_____ 5. Alfred Baumeler	e. pastry chef in Manhattan, emigrated in 1970 from the Dominican Republic
_____ 6. Julie Horvath-Krol	f. emigrated from Peru as a child, now is a senior brand manager with a pharmaceuticals company in New Jersey

LANGUAGE AND LIFE / **UNIT 1**

_____ 7. Paul Mak

g. president of the Brooklyn Chinese-American Association, came here in 1970 from Hong Kong

_____ 8. Mona Sharma Sachar

h. lawyer for the City University of New York, emigrated from Haiti about 30 years ago

BUILDING WRITING SKILLS

SUMMARIZING

Summarizing is a good way to help you understand an article and identify the author's main ideas. When you summarize, you should reduce the article to its main points in a few clear, concise sentences. Do not include any of your own ideas or opinions.

In your own words, summarize the advice of each of the people interviewed in the article.

1. Sonia Urban: _____

_____

_____

2. Liam Benson: _____

_____

_____

3. Florence Moise-Stone: _____

_____

_____

4. Dame Babou: _____

_____

_____

5. Alfred Baumeler: _____

_____

_____

6. Julie Horvath-Krol: _____

_____

_____

7. Paul Mak: _____

_____

_____

8. Mona Sharma Sachar: _____

_____

_____

Suppose you were asked to help write a welcome guide for immigrants or international students coming to the United States or your country. Write five things that you think should be included in the guide.

1. _____

_____

2. _____

_____

3. _____

_____

4. _____

_____

5. _____

_____

Using a dictionary, write the part of speech for each word, the meaning as it is used in the article, any synonyms for the word, and a sentence to help you remember the meaning. For the last two items, choose words from the article that were unfamiliar to you.

1. descendant (¶1)

part of speech: _____

definition: _____

synonyms: _____

sentence: _____

_____

2. stage (¶6)

part of speech: _____

definition: _____

synonyms: _____

sentence: _____

_____

3. practical (¶8)

part of speech: _____

definition: _____

synonyms: _____

sentence: _____

_____

4. emigrate (¶10)

part of speech: _____

definition: _____

synonyms: _____

sentence: _____

_____

5. cling (¶17)

part of speech: _____

definition: _____

synonyms: _____

sentence: _____

_____

6. privilege (¶25)

part of speech: _____

definition: _____

synonyms: _____

sentence: _____

_____

FYi

There are approximately fifty different alphabets in use in the world today.

7. vast (¶29)

   part of speech: _____

   definition: _____

   synonyms: _____

   sentence: _____

   _____

8. consecutive (¶30)

   part of speech: _____

   definition: _____

   synonyms: _____

   sentence: _____

   _____

9. _____ (¶   )

   part of speech: _____

   definition: _____

   synonyms: _____

   sentence: _____

   _____

10. _____ (¶   )

   part of speech: _____

   definition: _____

   synonyms: _____

   sentence: _____

   _____

The following short passage is excerpted from *Lost in Translation: A Life in a New Language,* the autobiography of Eva Hoffman. Ms. Hoffman was born in Krakow, Poland, and immigrated at the age of thirteen to Vancouver, Canada. Read this passage, in which she describes her perception of some of the cultural differences between her native Poland and her new country. Read the passage and then discuss the questions that follow.

[handwritten margin notes]
— Describe ∨ cause + effect relationships
— Discuss ∨ informal language + tone
↑ this article compared ∨ formal
tone ↑∨ other article.

LOST IN TRANSLATION

By Eva Hoffman

My mother says I'm becoming "English." This hurts me, because I know she means I'm becoming cold. I'm no colder than I've ever been, but I'm learning to be less demonstrative. I learn this from a teacher who, after contemplating the gesticulations with which I help myself describe the digestive system of a frog, tells me to "sit on my hands and then try talking." I learn my new reserve from people who take a step back when we talk, because I'm standing too close, crowding them. Cultural distances are different, I later learn in a sociology class, but I know it already. I learn restraint from Penny, who looks offended when I shake her by the arm in excitement, as if my gesture had been one of aggression instead of friendliness. I learn it from a girl who pulls away when I hook my arm through hers as we walk down the street—this movement of friendly intimacy is an embarrassment to her.

I learn also that certain kinds of truth are impolite. One shouldn't criticize the person one is with, at least not directly. You shouldn't say, "You are wrong about that"—though you may say, "On the other hand, there is that to consider." You shouldn't say, "This doesn't look good on you," though you may say, "I like you better in that other outfit." I learn to tone down my sharpness, to do a more careful conversational minuet.

Perhaps my mother is right, after all; perhaps I'm becoming colder. After a while, emotion follows action, response grows warmer or cooler according to gesture. I'm more careful about what I say, how loud I laugh, whether I give vent to grief. The storminess of emotion prevailing in our family is in excess of the normal here, and the unwritten rules for the normal have their osmotic effect.[1]

1. Why do you think the author named her autobiography *Lost in Translation*? Do you think it is an appropriate title?

2. In what ways is the author becoming less demonstrative?

3. How is she learning her new reserve?

4. What did she learn about truth?

5. According to the author, what is the relationship between emotion and gesture?

Describe some of the cultural differences between your native country and English-speaking countries.

_____

_____

_____

_____

_____

_____

Throughout history languages have evolved and changed. It is a natural process that was taking place long before movies and television came along to hasten the absorption of foreign words into the vocabularies of languages around the world. As you read "A 'glorious mongrel,'" you will see how the English language grew.

BEFORE YOU READ

PREREADING ACTIVITY

1. Write down any words in your native language that you know have been absorbed into the English language.

_____   _____   _____

_____   _____   _____

_____   _____   _____

2. Make a list of English words that have been absorbed into your native language.

_____   _____   _____

_____   _____   _____

_____   _____   _____

BUILDING READING SKILLS

PREVIEWING

There are several steps you can take to improve your reading comprehension skills. One of the most important of these, **previewing**, is something you should do *before* you read the article. When you preview a text, you examine certain parts of it before you read it all the way through. You can gather clues about an article from its title, subtitle, pictures, captions, and headings. Previewing will give you a good idea of what you are about to read and how you should approach reading it.

Look at the title and subtitle of the article on pages 14–15. Think about what they mean. Look at the drawing and its caption. Then read the first sentence of every paragraph. Write a few sentences that predict what you think the article will be about.

_____

_____

_____

Now read the whole article carefully, and see how close your prediction is.

[handwritten annotations: tone—teasing (suggested) propaganda / What is u underlying metaphor? / English=prostitute]

A 'glorious mongrel'

The language that some Americans want to defend against foreign invasions is itself a multicultural smorgasbord of borrowed words.

By Gerald Parshall

1   Back in 1780, John Adams urged the creation of an American academy with a lofty mission—to keep the English language pure. The Continental Congress, preoccupied with other challenges (such as winning independence from Britain), let the proposal die. And wisely so. It would have been like giving a courtesan a chastity belt for her birthday. "The English language," as Carl Sandburg once observed, "hasn't got where it is by being pure." Not from the get go.

2   The language that many now seek to shore up against the babel of America's multicultural masses is a *smorgasbord* (Swedish) of words borrowed from foreign tongues. Three out of four words in the dictionary, in fact, are foreign born. Sometimes anglicized, sometimes not, many loan words are so familiar that most English speakers are aware of their

exotic origins only vaguely if at all. We can borrow *sugar* from a neighbor only because English borrowed the word from Sanskrit centuries ago. Ask your *pal* (Romany) to go to the *opera* (Italian), and he may prefer instead to go hunting in the *boondocks* (Tagalog), to play *polo* (Tibetan) or to visit the *zoo* (Greek) to test his *skill* (Danish) at milking a *camel* (Hebrew), after which he may need a *shampoo* (Hindi). Whether silly or scholarly, many sentences have equally rich lineages, illustrating Dorothy Thompson's *aphorism* (Greek) that English is a "glorious and imperial mongrel" (*mongrel*, fittingly, being pure English).

3   English itself is one of history's most energetic immigrants. Three northern European tribes, the Angles, the Saxons and the Jutes, got the enterprise started by invading Britain around A.D. 449. The Vikings arrived from Scandinavia in

A.D. 793 to mix it up, battle-ax against battle-ax, adverb against adverb. The Norse and Anglo-Saxon tongues melded, enriching the word hoard. Example: You *reared* a child (Anglo-Saxon) or *raised* a child (Norse). As every schoolchild used to know, the Norman French conquered England in 1066. The language of the Saxon peasantry then conquered the Norman aristocracy. The result was a tongue that kept its Germanic structure but took in a huge new vocabulary of French words and through it Latin and Greek terms. Traders, warriors, scholars, pirates and explorers all did their part to advance English's cosmopolitan destiny.

4 The language was happily spiced with words from 50 languages even before the opening of the New World offered fresh avenues. Americans quickly became known for their own coinages, the many "Americanisms" they invented—words like *groundhog, lightning rod, belittle* (minted by Thomas Jefferson), *seaboard*—new words for a new land. But American English also adopted American Indian terms, (mostly place names) and welcomed useful words brought across the water by immigrants. The Dutch supplied *pit* (as found in fruit) and *boss* (as found in the front office), *sleigh, snoop* and *spook.* Spanish supplied *filibuster* and *bonanza.* Yiddish enabled Americans to *kibitz schmucks* who sold *schlock* or made *schmaltz.*

Big dictionary

5 Today, after 1,500 years of promiscuous acquisitiveness, the vocabulary of English is vast. The Oxford English Dictionary lists more than 600,000 words; German has fewer than one third

that number, French fewer than one sixth. What makes English mammoth and unique is its great sea of synonyms, words with roughly the same meaning but different connotations, different levels of formality and different effects on the ear. Anglo-Saxon words are blunt, Latin words learned, French words musical. English speakers can calibrate the tone and meter of their prose with great precision. They may *end* (Anglo-Saxon), *finish* (French) or *conclude* (Latin) their remarks. A girl can be *fair* (Anglo-Saxon), *beautiful* (French) or *attractive* (Latin). A bully may evoke *fear* (Anglo-Saxon), *terror* (French) or *trepidation* (Latin).

6 Its depth and precision have helped make English the foremost language of science, diplomacy and international business—and the medium of T-shirts from Tijuana to Timbuktu. It is the native tongue of 350 million people and a second language for 350 million more. Half the books being published in the world are in English; so is 80 percent of the world's computer text. While Americans debate bilingualism, foreigners learn English. Its popularity is fed by U.S. wealth and power, to be sure. But Richard Lederer, author of *The Miracle of Language* and other books on the peculiarities of English, believes the language's "internationality" has innate appeal. Not only are English's grammar and syntax relatively simple, the language's sound system is flexible and "user friendly"—foreign words tend to be pronounced the same as in their original tongue. "We have the most cheerfully democratic and hospitable language that ever existed," Lederer says. "Other people recognize their language in ours."

The word *alphabet* is derived from the first two letters of the Greek alphabet, *alpha* and *beta.*

Circle the letter of the choice that best completes the sentence or answers the question.

1. The author uses the sentence "Ask your pal to go to the opera, and he may prefer instead to go hunting in the boondocks, to play polo or to visit the zoo to test his skill at milking a camel, after which he may need a shampoo," to show that _____ .
   a. English has too many foreign words
   b. English vocabulary is difficult to learn
   c. English is rich in words borrowed from other languages
   d. English is a pure language and should stay that way

2. According to the article, one reason that English is the foremost language of science, diplomacy, and business is _____ .
   a. the complexity of its grammar
   b. its tone and meter
   c. the peculiarities of its origins
   d. the depth and precision of its vocabulary

3. The author explains the history of the English language in _____ .
   a. paragraph 1
   b. paragraph 2
   c. paragraph 3
   d. paragraph 5

4. Which of the following people believed that the English language should be kept pure?
   a. Carl Sandburg
   b. John Adams
   c. Dorothy Thompson
   d. Richard Lederer

5. All of the following statements are true about English except _____ .
   a. it is spoken by 700 million people
   b. half of all published books are in English
   c. it has a smaller vocabulary than German
   d. 75 percent of words in the dictionary are foreign born   *par. 2*

6. The words *finish, beautiful,* and *terror* all have _____ origins.
   a. French
   b. Latin
   c. Greek
   d. Anglo-Saxon

7. *Groundhog, lightning rod, belittle,* and *seaboard* are examples of words
   _____ .

   a. supplied by the Dutch and Spanish
   b. invented by Americans
   c. adopted from American Indian terms
   d. welcomed by immigrants

8. According to the author, English has such a vast vocabulary because it

   _____ .

   a. is a relatively new language
   b. is used in international business
   c. is easy to learn
   d. borrowed words from many languages

BUILDING READING SKILLS

SCANNING FOR DETAILS

Scanning is a technique that helps you locate information in an article quickly. When you scan, your eyes move quickly across the printed lines without reading every word.

Look only for the specific piece of information you need in order to answer a question or complete a task.

Scan the article to find the derivation of the following words. Then complete the chart.

WORD	LANGUAGE OF ORIGIN
1. raised	
2. reared	
3. zoo	
4. conclude	
5. boondocks	
6. skill	
7. bonanza	
8. trepidation	
9. camel	
10. aphorism	
11. schlock	
12. opera	
13. shampoo	
14. fear	

BUILDING READING SKILLS

EXAMINING MEANING

Read each of the following sentences from the article carefully. Then circle the letter of the sentence that is closest in meaning to the original.

1. *Sometimes anglicized, sometimes not, many loan words are so familiar that most English speakers are aware of their exotic origins only vaguely if at all.*

   a. Most English speakers are not fully aware of the origins of many familiar loan words.
   b. Anglicized and nonanglicized English speakers are sometimes aware of the exotic origins of familiar loan words.
   c. Many loan words are so familiar that most English speakers are aware of their exotic origins.

2. *The result was a tongue that kept its Germanic structure but took in a huge new vocabulary of French words and through it Latin and Greek terms.*

   a. The result was a language with a Germanic structure but without its rich vocabulary of French, Greek, and Latin words.
   b. The language that resulted had kept its original Germanic structure and French vocabulary.
   c. The new language retained its Germanic structure but incorporated many French words that included Latin and Greek terms.

3. *What makes English mammoth and unique is its great sea of synonyms, words with roughly the same meaning but different connotations, different levels of formality and different effects on the ear.*

   a. Several things account for the size of the English language, including synonyms, words with the same meaning and different levels of connotations, formality, and effects on the ear.
   b. English is mammoth and unique because of its great number of synonyms.
   c. Why does its great sea of synonyms make English a mammoth and unique language?

4. *Not only are English's grammar and syntax relatively simple, the language's sound system is flexible and "user friendly"—foreign words tend to be pronounced the same as in their original tongue.*

   a. The grammar and syntax of English are easy, and its sound system is flexible and easy to use.
   b. English's grammar and syntax are relatively simple, but its sound system isn't flexible or easy to use.
   c. Only English has a grammar and syntax that are simple and a sound system that is flexible and easy to use.

EXPANDING VOCABULARY

Using a dictionary, write the part of speech for each word, the meaning as it is used in the article, any synonyms for the word, and a sentence to help you remember the meaning. For the last three items, choose words from the article that were unfamiliar to you.

1. vaguely (¶2)

   part of speech: _____

   definition: _____

   synonyms: _____

   sentence: _____

   _____

2. lineage (¶2)

   part of speech: _____

   definition: _____

   synonyms: _____

   sentence: _____

   _____

Zeke Zzzyzus added the third "z" to the beginning of his surname so that his name would be the last entry in the Montreal, Canada, phone book.

3. mongrel (¶2)

   part of speech: _____

   definition: _____

   synonyms: _____

   sentence: _____

   _____

4. mammoth (¶5)

   part of speech: _____

   definition: _____

   synonyms: _____

   sentence: _____

   _____

5. connotation (¶5)

part of speech: _____

definition: _____

synonyms: _____

sentence: _____

_____

6. peculiarity (¶6)

part of speech: _____

definition: _____

synonyms: _____

sentence: _____

_____

7. innate (¶6)

part of speech: _____

definition: _____

synonyms: _____

sentence: _____

_____

8. _____ (¶   )

part of speech: _____

definition: _____

synonyms: _____

sentence: _____

_____

9. _____ (¶   )

part of speech: _____

definition: _____

synonyms: _____

sentence: _____

_____

10. _____ (¶   )

part of speech: _____

definition: _____

synonyms: _____

sentence: _____

_____

Read the following article about research into the differences in the ways that children and adults learn languages.

BREAKTHROUGH

THE BILINGUAL BRAIN

When Karl Kim immigrated to the United States from Korea as a teenager ten years ago, he had a hard time learning English. Now he speaks it fluently, and recently he had a unique opportunity to see how our brains adapt to a second language. Kim is a graduate student in the lab of Joy Hirsch, a neuroscientist at Memorial Sloan-Kettering Cancer Center in New York. He and Hirsch have recently found evidence that children and adults don't use the same parts of the brain when learning a second language.

The researchers used an instrument called a functional magnetic resonance imager to study the brains of two groups of bilingual people. One group consisted of those who had learned a second language as children. The other consisted of people who, like Kim, learned their second language later in life. When placed inside the MRI scanner, which allowed Kim and Hirsch to see which parts of the brain were getting more blood and were thus more active, people from both groups were asked to think about what they had done the day before, first in one language and then the other. (They couldn't speak out loud, because any movement would disrupt the scanning.)

Kim and Hirsch looked specifically at two language centers in the brain—Broca's area, in the left frontal part, which is believed to manage speech production, and Wernicke's area, in the rear of the brain, thought to process the meaning of language. Both groups of people, Kim and Hirsch found, used the same part of Wernicke's area no matter what language they were speaking. But their use of Broca's area differed.

People who learned a second language as children used the same region in Broca's area for both languages. But those who learned a second language later in life made use of a distinct region in Broca's area for their second language—near the one activated for their native tongue. How does Hirsch explain this difference? "When language is being hard-wired during development," says Hirsch, "the brain may intertwine sounds and structures from all languages into the same area." But once that wiring is complete, the management of a new language, with new sounds and structures, must be taken over by a different part of the brain.

A second possibility is simply that we may acquire languages differently as children than we do as adults. "If you watch mothers or family members teaching an infant to speak," says Hirsch. "it's very tactile, it's very auditory, it's very visual. There are a lot of different inputs. And that's very different from sitting in a classroom."[2]

BUILDING WRITING SKILLS

SUMMARIZING

Write a one-paragraph summary of the main ideas of the article above.

_____

_____

_____

_____

_____

_____

_____

_____

_____

Sandra Cisneros is a best-selling author whose writing draws on her Latino heritage. She is best known for her award-winning book of short stories, *The House on Mango Street,* which has been translated into seven languages and has sold more than half a million copies. "My Name" is one of the stories from *The House on Mango Street.* In this vignette, the main character tells us in her own simple but evocative language how she feels about her name.

BEFORE YOU READ

PREREADING DISCUSSION

1. It is through our names that we introduce ourselves to the world. How do you feel about your name? Do you like it? Have you ever thought about changing it? What would you change your name to?

2. Is there a story behind your name? In other words, did your parents give you that name for a reason, or was it just because they liked the name?

3. Does your name have a special meaning? What is it?

My Name

BY SANDRA CISNEROS

1   In English my name means hope. In Spanish it means too many letters. It means sadness, it means waiting. It is like the number nine. A muddy color. It is the Mexican records my father plays on Sunday mornings when he is shaving, songs like sobbing.

2   It was my great-grandmother's name and now it is mine. She was a horse woman too, born like me in the Chinese year of the horse—which is supposed to be bad luck if you're born female—but I think this is a Chinese lie because the Chinese, like the Mexicans, don't like their women strong.

3   My great-grandmother. I would've liked to have known her, a wild horse of a woman, so wild she wouldn't marry until my great-grandfather threw a sack over her head and carried her off. Just like that, as if she were a fancy chandelier. That's the way he did it.

4   And the story goes she never forgave him. She looked out the window all her life, the way so many women sit their sadness on an elbow. I wonder if she made the best with what she got or was she sorry because she couldn't be all the things she wanted to be. Esperanza. I have inherited her name, but I don't want to inherit her place by the window.

⁵ At school they say my name funny as if the syllables were made out of tin and hurt the roof of your mouth. But in Spanish my name is made out of a softer something, like silver, not quite as thick as sister's name Magdalena which is uglier than mine. Magdalena who at least can come home and become Nenny. But I am always Esperanza.

⁶ I would like to baptize myself under a new name, a name more like the real me, the one nobody sees. Esperanza as Lisandra or Maritza or Zeze the X. Yes. Something like Zeze the X will do.

● ●

HOW WELL DID YOU READ?

1. What does the narrator's name mean in English?

_____ *hope* _____

2. What does her name mean in Spanish?

_____ *too many letter* _____

3. Who was the narrator named after?

_____ *great grandmoth* _____

4. Why doesn't she like her name?

_____ *classmate say I funny* _____
_____ *no short form* _____

5. What does she wonder about her great-grandmother's life?

Did she make her life, was she sorry because she couldn't (handwritten)

6. What would she like to change her name to? Why?

Esperanza Martya Zeze v X (handwritten)

7. Why are both the narrator and her great-grandmother called "horse woman"?

Born in year of horse (handwritten)

8. What does she think about her sister's name?

ugly, lucky 6 H short form (handwritten)

TALK IT OVER

DISCUSSION

1. In your culture, how are children's names chosen? Is it common to name children after relatives? Do names have religious or historical significance?

2. In your family, are there any names that are passed down from one generation to the next?

3. In the story, the narrator's sister is nicknamed "Nenny." Do you have a nickname? Are nicknames common in your culture? How do people usually get their nicknames?

4. Do you think that a person's name influences his or her personality? Give examples to support your opinion.

5. Do you think that Esperanza can escape her great-grandmother's fate by changing her name to Zeze the X? Why or why not?

6. Does a person's name affect your first impression of that person? Can your impression change if that person changes his or her name? What examples can you give from "My Name" or from your own experience?

How do people's names develop and change with the passage of time? Read this excerpt from *The Play of Words* by Richard Lederer to learn about the ways that English names have evolved.

THE EVOLUTION OF ENGLISH NAMES

By Richard Lederer

The pattern of naming in the English language began with single names because, when people lived together in small communities, the supply of names was large enough so that none had to be repeated in the same tribe or group. Most first names are very old. Girls have been named Mary ("star of the sea") and boys John ("gift of God") for many centuries, and these remain, despite fads, the most popular first names in English-speaking countries.

As social groups grew larger, single names began popping up more often, and a system of distinguishing among people with the same first names had to be invented. Thus, villagers began to add a bit of descriptive information to the given name, and that's how we got last names, or surnames. The *sur* in the word comes from the Latin *super* and means "above and beyond."

Some of these surnames began life as descriptions of a person's coloring—Black, White, and Reid (Red); size—Small, Little, Longfellow; geography—Churchill, Rivers, York; or personal qualities—Smart, Wise, and Swift. A teetotaler might have picked up the name Drinkwater, a man of great strength Armstrong, and a loyal friend Truman.

Other names are patronymics and matronymics, family names derived from a parent or ancestor. Your name is probably one of these if it begins with Mc, Mac, O', or Fitz, or ends with son, sen, ov, or ovich, all of which mean "son of."

The largest category of surnames began as descriptions of the work people did. In the telephone directories of the world's English-speaking cities, Smith, which means "worker," is the most popular last name by a large margin over its nearest competitors, Jones and Johnson (both of which are patronymics). And it is no wonder when you consider that the village smith, who made and repaired all objects of metal, was the most important person in the community. International variations on Smith include Smythe, Schmidt, Smed, Faber, Ferrier, LeFebre, Ferraro, Kovacs, Manx, Goff, and Gough.[3]

BUILDING WRITING SKILLS

SUMMARIZING

Write a one-paragraph summary of the main ideas of the article above.

_____

_____

_____

_____

_____

_____

_____

_____

_____

RESPOND IN WRITING

A. Write a paragraph about your name. Use your answers to the prereading questions on page 23 as the basis of your paragraph. Add any other ideas you got from "My Name," from "The Evolution of English Names," and from listening to classmates talk about their names.

_____

_____

_____

_____

_____

_____

_____

_____

_____

B. In small groups, read your paragraph aloud and answer any questions that the people in your group might ask.

A Hungarian proverb says that a child who is loved has many names. Nicknames are a sign of affection. Each of the following names has many nicknames. Talk to North Americans and find out as many nicknames as you can for each of these names.

Margaret: _____

William: _____

Elizabeth: _____

Charles: _____

Catherine: _____

Richard: _____

Victoria: _____

Andrew: _____

In 1898, the most popular names in the United States were:

Mary
Margaret
Rose
Esther
Frances
Catherine
Annie
Marie
Sarah
Ida

John
Charles
Joseph
James
Francis
William
George
Edward
Louis
Samuel

BUILDING READING SKILLS

INCREASING READING SPEED

To be a good reader, it is important that you read as quickly and efficiently as possible. To increase your reading speed and efficiency, it is important to recognize words quickly. The following exercise will give you practice in quick word recognition. This is a timed exercise. You will have 20 seconds in which to underline the word that is the same as the first word in each line.

Example:

<u>is</u>	was	if	fit	<u>is</u>	in
1. when	new	hen	never	when	where
2. mild	wild	while	mild	mile	milk
3. dime	mime	dial	time	dime	fine
4. pit	pat	pit	pot	tin	pen
5. which	where	when	which	ditch	while
6. breathe	breath	breather	breathe	breadth	brave
7. cherry	cheery	church	cherish	cherry	change
8. change	clang	name	climate	grange	change
9. guest	ghost	aghast	again	guest	ghastly
10. stop	stop	top	tops	store	steal
11. sun	sing	nut	sun	sting	sung
12. kitten	kind	mitten	cat	king	kitten
13. forget	forge	forgot	forget	foreign	form
14. tree	trunk	treasure	tree	tell	ten
15. thick	thicken	this	thick	thin	trick

When you have finished, figure out how many answers you got right and check the appropriate box on page 263 in order to keep track of your progress.

In 1998, the most popular names in the United States were:

Jessica
Jennifer
Melissa
Ashley
Amanda
Samantha
Stephanie
Nicole
Tiffany
Christina

Michael
Christopher
Daniel
David
Matthew
Andrew
Jonathan
Anthony
Joseph
John[4]

FREEWRITING

When you think of the word *friendship*, what comes to mind? *Freewriting* is a technique that helps you find a focus when you are going to write on a broad topic. When you freewrite, write as much as you can as fast as you can without worrying about mistakes.

On a separate piece of paper, freewrite for 10 minutes on the topic of *friendship*.

Now read the following essay in which Ian Baker discusses his ideas about friendship.

FRIENDSHIP

By Ian Baker

I first met Joe Gans when we were both nine years old, which is probably the only reason he's one of my best friends. If I had first met Joe as a freshman in high school, we wouldn't even have had the chance to get to know each other. Joe is a day student, but I am a boarding student and under the general arbitrarily-based categorization of school-based social groups, we fall about as far apart as possible. We haven't been in the same classes, sports, or extracurricular activities.

Nonetheless, I spend nearly every weekend at his house and we talk on the phone every night. This is not to say that we would not have been compatible if we had first met in our freshman year. Rather, we just would not have been likely to spend enough time getting to know each other due to the lack of immediately visible mutual interests. In fact, to be honest, I struggle even now to think of things we have in common. But maybe that's what makes us enjoy each other's company so much. Maybe, for example, it's the theological arguments between an atheist (Joe) and a Buddhist (me) that make it interesting.

When I look at my friendship with Joe, I wonder how many people I've known whom I never disliked, but simply didn't take the time to get to know. Thanks to Joe, I have realized how little basis there is for the social divisions that exist in every community. Since this realization, I have begun to make an even more concerted effort to find friends in unexpected people and places.

I do not know if it is because nine-year-olds don't notice the differences among people that would keep them from making friends, or whether they are too young to even know that those differences exist. But I know that the first time I saw Joe Gans, I only saw a kid who might be looking for a friend. And it may seem strange, but ever since I realized all this, I've decided to make my friends the same way a nine-year-old would.

TALK IT OVER

DISCUSSION

1. Do you tend to make friends who are similar to, or different from, you?

2. Why does the author think young people are more open-minded about making friends? Do you agree with him?

3. The author made a friend who was different from him. Have you ever had a close friend from a different country, religion, race, background, or political ideology? What did you learn from that person?

4. Have you ever been friendly with someone who is much older or younger than you?

POSTREADING

DISCUSSION

1. What do you think you would like most and least about living in another country?

2. For some people, their name is a "numbing blow from which they never recover" (Marshall McLuhan). Are you one of those people? Is anyone you know?

3. One of Shakespeare's most frequently quoted passages is from *Romeo and Juliet*:

   What's in a Name? That which we call a rose,
   By any other name would smell as sweet.
   What does the passage mean? Do you agree with Shakespeare?

4. Are you bilingual? What are the advantages of being bilingual? Can you think of any disadvantages?

5. Look back at the passage from *Lost in Translation* on page 11. Do you think the people of your country are cold or warm? Why?

JUST FOR FUN

REBUS

A *rebus* is a kind of visual puzzle with words. It is the representation of words and phrases in the form of pictures, letters, or symbols. Use your imagination to solve the following rebuses and find the familiar word or expression. Then check the answer key on page 263.

Example: TI · ME can be read as a point in time.

1. When written vertically, T becomes _____.

   O
   W
   N

2.

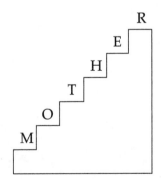

   _____

3. 1. D
   2. R
   3. A
   4. C   _____
   5. U
   6. L
   7. A

4. 6S5A4F3E2T1Y   _____

5. Now in here   _____

6. <u>Shirt</u>   _____

7. S   S
   I   I
   D   D   _____
   E   E

8. COF FEE   _____

Shoe

READER'S JOURNAL

Choose a topic that relates to the readings in this unit, and write for about ten to twenty minutes. Consider using one of the quotes or one of the discussion questions in this unit as the basis for your writing.

READER'S JOURNAL

Date: _____

POLAR
CONNECTIONS

Selections

"Antarctica is not a country, province, or territory, but a huge icecap (about the size of the United States and Mexico combined) governed by an international treaty and set aside exclusively for peaceful, scientific research . . . there are no native inhabitants—and anyone who comes is truly an 'alien' who could not survive without special clothing and shelter to wield off the terrible elements."[1]

Although it has no permanent settlements, Antarctica has been the subject of intense exploration since 1820. In addition, every year more and more tourists travel there. The readings in this unit will give you insight into the attraction this region holds for both scientists and tourists.

POINTS TO PONDER

DISCUSSION

Think about and then discuss the following questions.

1. Most of us live in the middle latitudes. Have you ever visited the North or South Pole, or do you know anyone who has?

2. Have you read any books or magazine articles about expeditions to either pole?

3. In small groups, make a list of the things you know about the Arctic and Antarctic regions in general and/or about the research that is taking place there.

_____

_____

_____

_____

_____

_____

Jeff Rubin, author of "Antarctica: A Travel Survival Kit" was born and raised in Michigan. He first visited Antarctica in 1987 while writing a story for *Time* magazine about Australia's Antarctic science program. Since then, he has returned to the continent nearly a dozen times as a lecturer and tour guide. As you read the introduction to his book, think about what it would be like to visit this cold continent.

BEFORE YOU READ

PREREADING DISCUSSION

1. Are you interested in adventure travel? If so, what kinds of adventures do you like?

2. If you could travel anywhere in the world, would Antarctica be on your list of places to visit? Why or why not?

3. What is the most beautiful place you have ever visited?

Antarctica

a lonely planet travel survival kit

By Jeff Rubin

1   Antarctica is one of the most beautiful places on earth. Its gigantic icebergs and ice shelves are found nowhere else on the globe. Its vast mountain ranges and the enormous emptiness of the polar plateau boggle the mind.

2   Antarctica is still very difficult to reach. The most isolated continent, it must be earned, either through a long, often uncomfortable ship voyage or an expensive airplane flight. Weather and ice—not clocks or calendars—set the schedule, and Antarctic tour companies always emphasize that their itineraries are completely at the mercy of the continent's changing moods.

3   Little wonder. Antarctica's wind speeds top 320 km/h, its temperatures plunge as low as -89°C, and its average precipitation is comparable to that of the driest deserts. These superlatives merely confirm that Antarctica is a spectacular wilderness, a wilderness of landscapes reduced to a pure haiku of ice, rock, water and sky, filled with wildlife still unafraid of humans.

Icebreaker *Kapitan Khlebnikov* near Balleny Islands

4   But Antarctica is a wilderness in a far greater sense than the mere fact that it has no indigenous people and even today remains all but unpopulated. Antarctica is also a wilderness of the mind. Traveling there is like visiting no other country. At times in Antarctica, the activities of the rest of humanity seem utterly insignificant; your ship or camp or research station becomes a world unto itself. Indeed, the personnel handbook issued by one national government funding research in Antarctica talks about "when you return to the world."

5   No one owns Antarctica, and no one ever should. The place is too big to belong to any single nation. The international treaty that governs Antarctica works so unprecedentedly well not merely because it has been carefully crafted by consensus, but also because Antarctica's real value lies in no animal, mineral or vegetable riches that can be extracted from it. The conti-nent's true wealth, the nations of the world appear to agree, lies in the continuation of its unique status as a free, open, unmilitarized land of international cooperation, scientific research and unsullied beauty.

6   The first tourists to reach the Antarctic continent did not arrive until 1957, when a Pan American flight from Christchurch (New Zealand) landed briefly at McMurdo Sound. Its lucky passengers bought the chance to see a tiny portion of the frozen 14.25 million sq km continent that until then had been the sole domain of sealers, whalers, explorers, scientists and soldiers—nearly all of them men. Antarctic tourism only really got under way in 1966 when Lars-Eric Lindblad began offering well-heeled visitors a chance to see The Ice on an annual basis.

7   Some people come to Antarctica simply to "bag" their seventh continent, or to check off one more destination on

their roster of obscure places. But it is also true that most Antarctic cruises contain a high percentage of repeat visitors. Antarctica, as one tour leader puts it, is "highly addictive."

8 Tourism to Antarctica has increased tremendously during the past decade. The collapse of the Soviet Union has forced cash-strapped research institutes to lease their ships in order to earn hard currency. And as word of mouth has spread news of the continent's beauty, demand has risen steeply. Today, the variety of Antarctic travel itineraries, activities and prices is wider than ever before, making the present the perfect time to head south . . . to the Far South.

9 Antarctica's growth industry has turned out to be tourism, not mining or oil drilling, as many people once feared. Tourists come to Antarc-tica to experience a clean white continent unlike any other. Provided that their visits are properly managed, these tourists just might, paradoxically, turn out to be one of the best assurances that this vast wilderness remains (nearly) as pure as the driven snow. Let us hope!

HOW WELL DID YOU READ?

A. **Read the following statements. If a statement is true, write *T* on the line. If it is false, write *F*.**

_____ 1. Antarctica is an isolated and difficult-to-reach continent.

_____ 2. Antarctica often experiences periods of heavy rainfall.

_____ 3. Several groups of indigenous people have made Antarctica their home.

_____ 4. Antarctica does not belong to any single country.

_____ 5. Tourism in Antarctica began in the early 1900s.

_____ 6. People travel to Antarctica for a variety of reasons.

_____ 7. Antarctica's biggest growth industries are mining and oil-drilling.

B. **Circle the letter of the choice that best completes the sentence or answers the question.**

1. The author writes about Antarctica in a tone of _____ .

   a. detachment and straightforwardness
   b. bitterness and regret
   c. admiration and awe
   d. fear and uncertainty

2. The primary purpose of this passage is to _____.

    a. entertain readers with amusing stories about Antarctica
    b. persuade readers to change the political status of Antarctica
    c. inform readers about the natural beauty and wonders of Antarctica
    d. explain the benefits of scientific research in Antarctica to readers

3. Which of the following topics is NOT mentioned in the passage?

    a. climate
    b. tourism
    c. natural environment
    d. religion

4. According to the passage, tourism to Antarctica has _____ .

    a. increased significantly in the past ten years
    b. increased slightly in the past decade
    c. remained the same since 1966
    d. decreased dramatically

5. The author would support which of the following conclusions?

    a. Antarctica should be exploited for its mineral wealth.
    b. Antarctica's animals and minerals should be left alone.
    c. Research institutes in Antarctica should be closed down.
    d. none of the above

**BUILDING
READING SKILLS**

UNDERSTANDING
POINT OF VIEW

Put a check mark next to the statements you think the author would agree with.

_____ 1. The natural wonders of Antarctica are awe inspiring.

_____ 2. Antarctica's unpredictable climate makes it difficult to plan travel there.

_____ 3. It is not important to ensure the continuation of Antarctica's unique status as a free unmilitarized zone.

_____ 4. Many people who visit Antarctica want to return there again.

_____ 5. There should be an increase in the amount of mining and oil-drilling in Antarctica.

_____ 6. Traveling to Antarctica is similar to visiting many other countries.

BUILDING READING SKILLS

FACT VERSUS OPINION

Read the following statements. If a statement is a fact (something that has been proven), write *FACT* on the line. If a statement is an opinion (ideas or beliefs that have not been proven), write *OPINION* on the line.

_____ 1. Antarctica is one of the most beautiful places on earth.

_____ 2. Wind speeds in Antarctica can reach over 320 km/h.

_____ 3. Antarctica is governed by an international treaty.

_____ 4. The true wealth of Antarctica depends on the continuation of its unique status.

_____ 5. The first tourists reached Antarctica in 1957.

_____ 6. Antarctica's primary growth industry is tourism.

TALK IT OVER

DISCUSSION

1. What kinds of people do you think Antarctica attracts?

2. How many continents have you visited? Which ones?

3. The author describes Antarctica as "one of the most beautiful places on earth." Does Antarctica match your definition of beauty? What makes Antarctica so beautiful for the author? What makes a place beautiful for you?

4. The author writes "Antarctica is also a wilderness of the mind." What do you think he means by that statement?

EXPANDING VOCABULARY

Using a dictionary, write the part of speech for each word, the meaning as it is used in the article, any synonyms for the word, and a sentence to help you remember the meaning. For the last two items, choose words from the article that were unfamiliar to you.

1. gigantic (¶1)

part of speech: _____

definition: _____

synonyms: _____

sentence: _____

_____

2. plunge (¶3)

part of speech: _____

definition: _drop; descend (precipitously) to_____

synonyms: _____

sentence: _____

_____

3. indigenous (¶4)

part of speech: _____

definition: _native_____

synonyms: _____

sentence: _____

_____

4. extract (¶5)

part of speech: _____

definition: _take out_____

synonyms: _____

sentence: _____

_____

5. unique (¶5)

part of speech: _____

definition: _'one'_____

synonyms: _____

sentence: _____

_____

6. domain (¶6)

part of speech: _____

definition: _province / zone_____

synonyms: _____

sentence: _____

_____

7. obscure (¶7)

part of speech: _____

definition: ___*not obvious*_____

synonyms: _____

sentence: _____

_____

8. collapse (¶8)

part of speech: _____

definition: ___*fall apart*_____

synonyms: _____

sentence: _____

_____

9. _____ (¶   )

part of speech: _____

definition: _____

synonyms: _____

sentence: _____

_____

10. _____ (¶   )

part of speech: _____

definition: _____

synonyms: _____

sentence: _____

_____

BUILDING READING SKILLS

EXAMINING LANGUAGE

The descriptive language in Selection 1 brings the Antarctic landscape to life. In small groups, identify the phrases that paint particularly vivid pictures of the way Antarctica looks. Underline those phrases in the text and discuss them with your class as a whole.

Groups.   Find particularly descriptive phrases.

Explain the "joke"

RESPOND IN WRITING

Suppose you were asked to write a travel guide to your country. What kinds of information would you include in the introduction to get your readers excited about visiting your country? Make a list.

_____

_____

_____

_____

_____

_____

_____

_____

Use your list to help you write the introduction to your travel guide.

_____

_____

_____

_____

_____

_____

_____

_____

There are several kinds of penguins, but all of them live in the Southern Hemisphere. Some live on the ice in the Antarctic, and others live farther north in New Zealand, Australia, South Africa, and the Galapagos Islands. They live only in areas touched by cold sea currents from Antarctica and never move into areas where the ocean water is warmer. Most species of penguins live in colonies called *rookeries*. Read "Survival of the Coldest" to learn more about these fascinating birds.

BEFORE YOU READ

PREREADING DISCUSSION

1. Have you ever seen penguins at a zoo or aquarium?

2. How do you feel about the idea of zoos and aquariums? What are your thoughts on keeping animals apart from their natural habitats?

Survival of the Coldest

By Jeff Rubin

1   Human life, British philosopher Thomas Hobbes famously declared, is "nasty, brutish, and short." The same is true of the life of the penguin. On my trips to Antarctica as a tour guide and an author, that landscape's frigid temperatures and fierce winds have impressed upon me that for the animals living there, emotion is an unaffordable luxury. The cold calculus of Darwinian struggle requires that survival be the first and final determinant of appearance and behavior.

2   Of the 17 species of modern penguins, four breed on the Antarctic continent: Adélies, chinstraps, emperors, and gentoos. A fifth, the rockhopper, breeds on the subantarctic islands surrounding Antarctica. Few creatures lend themselves quite so easily to anthropomorphism as these birds. But as much as penguins may resemble dinner-jacketed bankers, many scientists believe the birds' coloration has evolved as a means of camouflage. Their black backs blend in with the dark-blue Southern Ocean, while underwater their white breasts are difficult to pick out when seen from below, against a background of ice floes and sunlit sky.

3   Form follows function in other ways. With their streamlined shape

Adélie Penguin

moment of a penguin's life. On land, skuas, sheathbills, and giant petrels snatch eggs and chicks left unattended. The predators often compete; to watch two skuas in a tug-of-war over a bedraggled but still-living chick is to witness nature at its rawest.

5 At sea, leopard seals and killer whales grab the first bird that takes the plunge. Penguins crowd together on icebergs and coastal cliffs, moving forward to literally force those in front to test the waters with their very lives.

6 Penguins' breeding biology can be equally brutal. In a reproductive heir-and-the-spare strategy, some species, such as the rockhoppers, lay and hatch two eggs—with the goal of raising just one healthy chick to adulthood. In the likely event that death intervenes in the case of the heir, the spare is ready. If, however, both chicks manage to survive, parents must begin to favor their designated heir.

7 First-time visitors to a rookery are often upset by the sight of a scrawny, underfed spare crying feebly beside a fat, healthy sibling. "Can't we do something?" tourists have pleaded with me as I've guided them through these colonies. No, I tell them, there is nothing we can do. The penguins have their own way of surviving.

and paddle-like wings, penguins are ideally adapted for underwater "flight." As bird bones go, penguins' are unusually solid and heavy, helping the birds to remain submerged. Short, bristly feathers provide waterproofing, and thick down and a layer of blubber add insulation. Penguins are so well protected from the cold, in fact, that on sunny days they can actually become overheated.

4 Despite these adaptations, the danger of violent death lurks at every

---

SCANNING- TEAM COMPETITION

HOW WELL DID YOU READ?

A. Circle the letter of the choice that best completes the sentence or answers the question.

1. What does the author consider to be the most important determinant of the appearance and behavior of penguins?

'first & final'

    a. luxury
    b. survival
    c. length of life
    d. emotion

2. How many species of modern penguins breed on the Antarctic continent?

    a. 17
    b. none
    c. 5
    d. 4

3. Which of the following species do not breed on the Antarctic continent?

    a. Adélies
    b. gentoos
    c. rockhoppers
    d. emperors

4. Many scientists believe that the coloration of penguins evolved as a means of _____ .

    a. anthropomorphism   ~ Pronunciation   animals in human form
    b. camouflage   But,
    c. beauty
    d. insulation

5. Penguins are adapted well for underwater flight because of their _____ .

    a. short, bristly feathers
    b. thick down and a layer of blubber
    c. black backs and white breasts
    d. streamlined shape and paddle-like wings

6. Insulation for penguins is provided by their _____ .

    a. short, bristly feathers
    b. layer of blubber   meaning
    c. coloration
    d. paddle-like wings

7. For penguins, the danger of violent death is _____ .

    a. a constant threat   looks.
    b. a seasonal threat
    c. a rare occurrence
    d. an occasional problem

8. Some species of penguins use the heir-and-the-spare strategy to _____ .

    a. raise many healthy offspring
    b. feed their young
    c. ensure that one chick survives to adulthood
    d. none of the above

"There are a lot of misconceptions about penguins—that all of them are from the north; often, advertising that relates polar bears, Eskimos, and penguins is totally false, because all penguin species are from the Southern Hemisphere. You would never see a polar bear with a penguin, or an Eskimo with a penguin, because they live at opposite ends of the earth."[2]

47

B. Answer the following questions in complete sentences.

1. What does the author mean by "form follows function"?

   _____

   _____

2. What dangers do penguins face on land? At sea?

   _____

   _____

3. How do penguins force members of their group to "test the waters"? Why do they do it?

   _____

   _____

4. How does penguins' coloration act as camouflage?

   _____

   _____

5. What physical characteristics do penguins have that help them survive?

   _____

   _____

BUILDING READING SKILLS

EXAMINING MEANING

Read each of the following sentences from the article carefully. Then circle the letter of the sentence that is closest in meaning to the original.

1. *As bird bones go, penguins' are unusually solid and heavy . . .*

   a. Penguins have more solid and heavier bones than most other birds.
   b. Bird bones are usually solid and heavy.
   c. Compared to other birds, penguins are unusually light.

2. *Few creatures lend themselves quite so easily to anthropomorphism as these birds.*

   a. A few of these birds lend themselves easily to anthropomorphism.
   b. These birds are more anthropomorphic than most other animals.
   c. These birds are not as anthropomorphic as most other creatures.

3. *But much as penguins may resemble dinner-jacketed bankers, many scientists believe the birds' coloration has evolved as a means of camouflage.*

   a. Penguins might look like bankers in formal clothes, but many scientists think that their coloration evolved as a means of camouflage.
   b. Both bankers and scientists agree that penguins' coloration evolved as a means of camouflage.
   c. Bankers disagree with scientists who believe that penguins' coloration evolved as a means of camouflage.

4. *Penguins are so well protected from the cold, in fact, that on sunny days they can actually become overheated.*

   a. Penguins stay cold even on sunny days.
   b. Penguins can get overheated from the sun because they are insulated from the cold.
   c. Penguins become overheated because they are not protected enough from the cold.

5. *Despite these adaptations, the danger of violent death lurks at every moment of a penguin's life.*

   a. Because of their adaptations, penguins usually escape violent death.
   b. The danger of violent death is a result of penguins' adaptations.
   c. Penguins' adaptations do not prevent them from being in constant danger of violent death.

EXPANDING VOCABULARY

Using a dictionary, write the part of speech for each word, the meaning as it is used in the article, any synonyms for the word, and a sentence to help you remember the meaning. For the last two items, choose words from the article that were unfamiliar to you.

1. frigid (¶1)

   part of speech: _____

   definition: _____

   synonyms: _____

   sentence: _____

   _____

2. resemble (¶2)

part of speech: _____

definition: _____

synonyms: _____

sentence: _____

_____

3. camouflage (¶2)

part of speech: _____

definition: _____

synonyms: _____

sentence: _____

_____

4. insulation (¶3)

part of speech: _____

definition: _____

synonyms: _____

sentence: _____

_____

5. lurk (¶4)

part of speech: _____

definition: _____

synonyms: _____

sentence: _____

_____

6. predator (¶4)

part of speech: _____

definition: _____

synonyms: _____

sentence: _____

_____

7. brutal (¶6)

part of speech: _____

definition: _____

synonyms: _____

sentence: _____

_____

8. heir (¶6)

part of speech: _____

definition: _____

synonyms: _____

sentence: _____

_____

9. _____ (¶   )

part of speech: _____

definition: _____

synonyms: _____

sentence: _____

_____

10. _____ (¶   )

part of speech: _____

definition: _____

synonyms: _____

sentence: _____

_____

Researchers have found bacteria thriving 6 to 8 feet below the surface of ice-covered lakes in the South Pole. This discovery suggests that life is possible on Mars or on Europa, a frozen moon of Jupiter.

Scientists want Congress to appropriate about $220 million for a high-tech research station to replace the deteriorating twenty-year-old one now in use at Antarctica. As you will read in "Cool Science on Antarctica," their projects include the study of life forms in a lake buried under the ice, penguin behavior, meteorite collection, and global warming.

BEFORE YOU READ

PREREADING DISCUSSION

1. It is said that Antarctica has the harshest climate on earth. Why would people want to go there to work or for pleasure?

2. Do you believe that polar exploration is worth the enormous outlay of time and money that go into it? How about space exploration? Do you think *that* is worth the time and money?

BUILDING READING SKILLS

SKIMMING

Skimming is a technique that helps you grasp the main idea of an article quickly. When you skim, do not worry about specific details since you are only reading for main ideas.

Read the article one time quickly for the main ideas. Then put a check mark next to the topics discussed in the article.

_____ ✓ 1. why Antarctica is a good place to study meteorites

_____ 2. how scientists collect specimens from our solar system

_____ ✓ 3. what scientists might learn from life forms in a lake buried beneath the polar ice

_____ ✓ 4. how scientists in Antarctica are using robots to help in their research

_____ 5. where penguins breed around the world

_____ ✓ 6. why the number of penguins that breed in Antarctica is decreasing

Now read the article again more carefully and do the exercises that follow it.

Cool Science on Antarctica

WHY DO SCIENTISTS FLOCK TO THE COLDEST, WINDIEST PLACE ON EARTH?

BY CHANA FREIMAN STIEFEL

Way down south, at the bottom of the globe, researchers at the South Pole Station are feeling low. Whipping winds and freezing temperatures have taken a toll on the 20-year-old complex. The dome-shaped building is sinking into a thick layer of snow. Power outages, fuel leaks, and sewage spills torment the 100 or more American scientists who live there during the "warmer" months.

Many of the researchers would like to replace their aging station with a $220-million high-tech structure. But some members of Congress want to cut back on Antarctic research. Why, they ask, should taxpayers spend so much money on such a remote continent?

Scientists have an answer: Because of its extreme conditions, Antarctica yields clues to our planet's past, present, and future. Right now, about 650 American researchers are flocking to Antarctica, as they do every September, to take advantage of the "balmy" spring and summer (-16 degrees C, or 4 degrees F, on a good day). After reading about some of their most interesting projects, ask yourself whether science in Antarctica is worth funding.

Meteorite Mania

Other than natural-history museums, Antarctica is the best place to hunt for meteorites, or space rocks that crash into Earth. Last year, geologist Ralph Harvey and his team from ANSMET (the Antarctic Search for Meteorites) found 390 meteorites.

"If you want to pick up things that fall to Earth, the obvious thing to do is lay out the biggest possible white sheet you can find," says Harvey, a professor at Case Western Reserve University in Cleveland, Ohio. That's what Antarctica is—a sheet of white-and-blue ice and snow the size of the United States and Mexico combined.

Meteorites peppering the surface of Antarctica are first covered by layers of snow. Packed in under pressure, the snow turns to ice. Over thousands of years, the ice spreads out toward the edges of the continent and usually breaks off as icebergs. Many meteorites encased in those icebergs float away, never to be seen again.

But some of Antarctica's mountain ranges (like the Transantarctic Mountains) block the flow of ice toward the sea. Dry air and winds of up to 144 kph (90 mph) turn the trapped ice into vapor—a process called sublimation. As the ice disappears, meteorites show up on the surface like chocolate chips in a cookie, just waiting to be scooped up by the ANSMET team.

Although Congress might find Antarctic research expensive, hunting for meteorites in Antarctica is the cheapest and safest way to collect specimens from our solar system—without heading to space. But Harvey and other meteorite hunters have only six to eight weeks a year to search. Even during Antarctica's summer, sudden blizzards slow researchers down.

Now scientists are planning to send a "meteorobot" to Antarctica to help in the search. The all-weather robot will be equipped with sensors to detect the chemical and magnetic signatures of meteorites. When it spots a possible meteorite, the robot will plant a flag in the ice so researchers know where to look.

Buried Lake

While some scientists explore the surface of Antarctica, others are learning more about a giant body of water 4 km (2.5 miles) beneath the ice pack.

Scientists first discovered Lake Vostock in the 1970s by using radio waves that penetrate the ice. Since then they have used sound waves and even satellites to map this massive body of water (14,000 sq. km, or 5,400 square miles).

How does the water in Lake Vostok remain liquid beneath an ice sheet? The thick glacier above acts like an insulating blanket and keeps the water from freezing, says Martin Siegert, a glaciologist from the University of Wales in Great Britain. In addition, geothermal heat from deep within the Earth may warm the hidden lake.

The scientists suspect that microbes may be living in Lake Vostok, closed off from the outside world for more than 2 million years. Anything found there will be totally alien to what's on the surface of Earth, says Siegert. Scientists are trying to find a way to drill into the ice and draw water samples without causing contamination. Again, robots might be the solution.

If all goes as planned, a drill-shaped cryorobot (<u>cryo</u> means cold), will melt through the surface ice. When it reaches the lake, it will release a hydrorobot (<u>hydro</u> means water) that can swim in the lake, take pictures, and look for signs of life.

The scientists hope their discoveries will shed light on life in outer space, which might exist in similar dark and airless conditions. Recently, close-up pictures of Jupiter's moon Europa showed signs of water beneath its icy surface. Once tested in Antarctica, cryorobots could be sent to Europa to search for life there, too.

Penguin Plunge

Meanwhile, a scientist at Montana State University has discovered that penguins in Antarctica are taking a plunge. In the mid-1980s, zoologist Wayne Trivelpiece found that 22 of every 100 Adélie penguins returned to their nesting grounds on King George Island to breed. Last year, he recorded only 10 of every 100 hatchlings returning—more than a 50 percent drop.

Why the decline? Trivelpiece suspects warmer weather. Winter temperatures on the island have risen 5.5 degrees C (19.9 degrees F) since the 1940s. The heat isn't frying the birds, but it does melt sea ice. As the ice disappears, so do algae that cling to it. Without algae to feed on, shrimplike creatures called krill die too. And krill are the mainstay of the penguins' diet.

Some scientists say warmer winters are natural—just a blip in the climate record. But Trivelpiece and others worry that the trend is a sign of global warming, a rise in Earth's temperature. Global warming may result from human activities such as burning fossil fuels (coal and oil) and cutting down rain forests. These actions release gases like carbon dioxide and methane into the atmosphere. The gases trap the Sun's heat and drive up temperatures.

Other scientists fear that global warming could melt an ice sheet in West Antarctica, releasing enough water to raise the world's oceans 6.25 meters (20 feet) or more and flood coastlines along Florida and elsewhere.

A. Read the following statements. If a statement is true, write *T* on the line.
If it is false, write *F*.

_____T_____ 1. Scientists believe that because of its extreme conditions, Antarctica can provide information about Earth's past, present, and future.

_____F_____ 2. Scientists in Antarctica are happy with their twenty-year-old research station.

_____T_____ 3. Hunting for meteorites in Antarctica is cheaper and safer than looking for them in space.

_____T_____ 4. Lake Vostok was discovered by using radio waves that penetrate the ice.

_____T_____ 5. Penguins mainly eat shrimplike creatures called krill.

_____F_____ 6. Gases such as carbon dioxide and methane trap the sun's heat and lower temperatures on Earth.

B. Match each term with its definition.

TERM	DEFINITION
__e__ 1. meteorites	a. robot that detects chemical and magnetic signatures of meteorites
__c__ 2. ANSMET	b. drill-shaped robot for melting through surface ice
__g__ 3. sublimation	c. the Antarctic Search for Meteorites
__a__ 4. meteorobot	d. coal and oil
__h__ 5. Lake Vostok	e. space rocks that crash to Earth
__b__ 6. cryorobot	f. robot that can swim and take pictures
__f__ 7. hydrorobot	g. process by which dry air and winds turn trapped ice into vapor
__d__ 8. fossil fuels	h. giant body of water beneath the ice pack

BUILDING READING SKILLS

FACT VERSUS THEORY

Read the following statements. If according to the article a statement is a fact (something that has been proven), write *FACT* on the line. If according to the article a statement is a theory (someone's idea or assumption that has not yet been proven), write *THEORY* on the line.

_____T_____ 1. Microbes may be living in Lake Vostok.

_____F_____ 2. There has been more than a 50 percent decrease in the number of Adélie penguins returning to breed in Antarctica.

_____T_____ 3. Warmer weather in Antarctica is causing fewer Adélie penguins to breed on King George Island.

_____T_____ 4. The rising winter temperatures in Antarctica can be interpreted as a sign of global warming.

_____F_____ 5. Winter temperatures in Antarctica have risen 5.5 degrees C since the 1940s.

_____T_____ 6. Global warming could melt an ice sheet in West Antarctica, raising the ocean level and causing flooding.

READ AND EXPLAIN

Explain the following scientific processes in your own words:

1. how the water in Lake Vostok remains liquid beneath the ice sheet

   a) glacier ice on top acts as an isulator
   b) heat from within earth warms Lake

2. how scientists are planning to study water samples from Lake Vostok

   a) drill thru ice w/ cryobot
   b) under ice, use hydrobot to swim in the lake + take pics

3. how meteorites covered by layers of snow can turn up on the surface thousands of years later

   a) covered by snow, b) snow covering turns to ice,
   c) ice moves to edges of continent d) ice flow is
   blocked by mountain ranges e) dry air + wind change ice to vapor

4. why Wayne Trivelpiece thinks warmer weather in Antarctica is affecting the breeding patterns of penguins (Explain the process.)

   _____

   _____

   f) ice disappears + meteorites are left behind.

EXPANDING VOCABULARY

Using a dictionary, write the part of speech for each word, the meaning as it is used in the article, any synonyms for the word, and a sentence to help you remember the meaning. For the last two items, choose words from the article that were unfamiliar to you.

1. torment (¶1)

   part of speech: _____

   definition: _____

   synonyms: _____

   sentence: _____

   _____

2. remote (¶2)

   part of speech: _____

   definition: _____

   synonyms: _____

   sentence: _____

   _____

3. specimen (¶8)

   part of speech: _____

   definition: _____

   synonyms: _____

   sentence: _____

   _____

4. blizzard (¶8)

   part of speech: _____

   definition: _____

   synonyms: _____

   sentence: _____

   _____

5. penetrate (¶11)

   part of speech: _____

   definition: _____

   synonyms: _____

   sentence: _____

   _____

6. massive (¶11)

   part of speech: _____

   definition: _____

   synonyms: _____

   sentence: _____

   _____

FYi

Ice Station SHEBA (Surface Heat Budget of the Arctic) is a six-nation research expedition that is studying the disappearing Arctic ice cap. Because this northernmost ice cap, which is roughly the size of the United States, is believed to act as a kind of giant conveyor belt that sends nutrients and fresh water to southerly oceans, there is great concern that it too may be melting because of carbon dioxide and other gases that trap heat.[5]

7. suspect (¶13)

   part of speech: _____

   definition: _____

   synonyms: _____

   sentence: _____

   _____

8. trend (¶17)

   part of speech: _____

   definition: _____

   synonyms: _____

   sentence: _____

   _____

9. _____ (¶   )

   part of speech: _____

   definition: _____

   synonyms: _____

   sentence: _____

   _____

10. _____ (¶   )

   part of speech: _____

   definition: _____

   synonyms: _____

   sentence: _____

   _____

**BUILDING
READING SKILLS**

UNDERSTANDING
POETRY

The **denotation** of a word is the dictionary definition of the word. Many words also have a **connotation**. This is a feeling or suggestion of additional meaning that the word gains from the context in which it is used. The connotation is an idea that the word makes you think of, rather than the actual meaning of the word. Poets often use connotations of language when they write.

Robert Frost (1874-1963) is one of the most important North American poets of the twentieth century. Frost was awarded the Pulitzer Prize for poetry four times, and in 1961, at the inauguration of President John F. Kennedy, he became the first poet to read one of his own poems at a presidential inauguration. Frost's poetry, with its emphasis on nature, is still immensely popular today.

Read the poem below and think about the connotations of fire and ice.

Fire and Ice

Some say the world will end in fire,
Some say in ice.
From what I've tasted of desire
I hold with those who favor fire.
But if it had to perish twice,
I think I know enough of hate
To say that for destruction ice
Is also great
And would suffice.[3]

TALK IT OVER

DISCUSSION

1. What do you think this poem is about?

2. What do the words *fire* and *ice* connote in this poem?

3. Who do you think Frost is referring to in line 1? In line 2?

4. How would you describe the tone of this poem?

**BUILDING
READING SKILLS**

INCREASING
READING SPEED

You will have 20 seconds in which to underline the word that is the same as the first word in each line.

1. glue	glum	gosh	galosh	glue	glow
2. moral	morale	morals	moped	moral	mope
3. proceed	process	proceed	proceeds	proctor	prom
4. crook	crooked	cross	crook	croon	crop
5. exam	exams	examine	extinct	examined	exam
6. bike	bilk	bill	bilge	bike	bile
7. equal	equal	even	event	equals	equally
8. mask	mast	mask	make	made	masks
9. real	reel	feel	reality	reed	real
10. peek	peer	peeked	pear	peek	peeve
11. heat	hear	heart	heat	heal	heave
12. miss	mist	misty	missile	mink	miss
13. pole	lope	lose	polite	pole	police
14. live	lice	living	lively	like	live
15. health	heart	hearty	healthy	hearth	health

When you have finished, figure out how many answers you got right and check the appropriate box on page 263 in order to keep track of your progress.

Scientists have many questions about the global effects of changes in climate. The massive ice sheets on Antarctica may hold answers to some of the questions. Read "Cracks in the Antarctic Ice," which takes a look at ice melts of the past and the uncertainties about ice melts in the future.

CRACKS IN THE ANTARCTIC ICE

By Laura Tangley

Among global warming's most frightening threats is the prediction that the polar ice caps will melt, raising sea levels so much that coastal cities from New York to Los Angeles to Shanghai will be inundated. Scientists agree that the key player in this scenario is the West Antarctic ice sheet, a Brazil-size mass of frozen water that's as much as 7,000 feet thick. Unlike floating ice shelves, which have little impact on sea level when they disintegrate, the ice sheet is anchored to bedrock well below the sea's surface. Surrounded by open ocean, it is also vulnerable. But Antarctic experts disagree strongly on just how unstable it is.

Now, new evidence reveals that all or most of the West Antarctic ice sheet collapsed at least once during the past 1.3 million years—a period when global temperatures probably were not significantly higher than they are today and the ice sheet was assumed to have been stable. In geologic time, a million years is recent history.

The proof, which was published last week in *Science*, comes from a team of glaciologists from Uppsala University in Sweden and the California institute of Technology in Pasadena, who drilled deep holes near the edge of the ice sheet. Within samples collected from sediments lying beneath the ice, they found fossils of microscopic marine plants called diatoms, which suggest that the region was not solid ice at the end of the Pleistocene Epoch but an open ocean. As Hermann

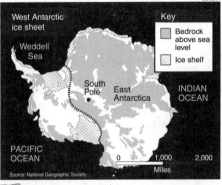

West Antarctic ice sheet

Weddell Sea

South Pole

East Antarctica

INDIAN OCEAN

PACIFIC OCEAN

USN&WR

Key

Bedrock above sea level

Ice shelf

0   1,000   2,000
Miles

Source: National Geographic Society

Engelhardt, a coauthor from Cal Tech, says, the West Antarctic ice sheet "has disappeared and can disappear again."

Of course, just because the ice sheet can disappear doesn't mean that it will. A host of unpredictable variables, from global temperature changes to how the ice sheet responds to the breakdown of surrounding ice shelves, will help determine its fate. One major uncertainty involves the ice streams that drain the massive sheet. Like ocean currents, these streams, which can be 90 miles across, move up to 100 times faster than the sheet that houses them, providing a mechanism for rapid ice loss. According to Engelhardt, one stream, called Ice Stream B, has been widening by 33 feet a year, a sign that the stream may be speeding up and the sheet breaking down. Other scientists, however, believe that the ice streams may be slowing.

Mysteries below. More uncertainty lies beneath the ice. It turns out that the behavior of ice streams may be strongly influenced by newly recognized, yet little understood, processes of subglacial geology. These findings, which were published in last week's *Nature*, will make it even harder to predict the ice sheet's future.

Still, few researchers would question the consequences of a meltdown: Antarctica contains 90 percent of Earth's ice and 70 percent of its fresh water. If the continent's vast western ice sheet slid into the ocean, it would raise sea levels by up to 20 feet worldwide.[4]

BUILDING WRITING SKILLS

SUMMARIZING

On a separate piece of paper, write a one-paragraph summary of the main ideas of the article above.

ORAL REPORT

The Arctic is a large, cold region around the North Pole. Unlike Antarctica, which is an ice-covered continent surrounded by oceans, the Arctic has a central ocean almost enclosed by land.

Research one of the following topics about the Arctic. Prepare a five-minute oral presentation for your class.

climate   vegetation   wildlife   people   explorers   scientific research

Read and discuss the following questions.

1. Author Sharon McAuliffe traveled to Antarctica in 1994. She reported seeing "some of the most spectacular icebergs and glaciers on Earth" and standing "on the edge of vast penguin colonies more than 100,000 birds strong." According to McAuliffe, "Venturing to Antarctica is like journeying to another planet right here on our own. It is a foreboding destination, where ice, often more than a mile thick, covers much of the surface and 200-mile-an-hour winds can relentlessly blow for days on end. . . . But nothing, not even the sight of an iceberg, quite prepares one for the stark, physical grandeur of the continent itself. It is another world without scale or dimension. I have no way to place this immense landscape into any context."[6] Would you like to travel to Antarctica? What would you be most interested in seeing there?

2. What does Wallace Broeker of Columbia University's Earth Observatory mean when he says, "Climate is an angry beast, and we are poking it with sticks."[7] What are some of the rampages we can expect from this "angry beast" if we push it too far?

3. Not only does climate affect human behavior, but human activity may also affect climate. In what ways does climate affect human behavior? In what ways do our activities affect the climate?

4. "The Arctic and Antarctic regions may be far away from us, but we ignore them at our peril."[8] Based on the readings in this unit and information from your oral reports, discuss the dangers.

Answer the following questions. Then check your answers on page 263.

1. Seven of the months in the year have 31 days. How many months have 28 days?

2. What five-letter word becomes shorter when you add two letters to it?

3. A black horse jumps over a tower and lands on a small man. The man then disappears. Where could this happen?

4. No matter how hungry they are, people in the Arctic regions would never eat penguin meat. Why not?

5. If you buy a car for $500, sell it for $700, buy it back for $800, and sell it for $900, how much is your profit?

6. There are two doors. Behind one of the doors is a dead end. Behind the other door is the path you are looking for. There is a guard in front of each door. One of the guards always tells the truth, but the other guard always lies. What question can you ask either guard so you can find out which door you should go through?

7. Look at the way the letters of the Roman alphabet are written below. Some of the letters are above the line and some are below it. Figure out the guideline and put the letter "Z" in the correct position.

<u>A   EF HI KLMN   T VWXY</u>

    BCD G   J   OPQRS U

8. Three sets of twins each have a garden. The twins' names are Daisy, Heather, Ivy, Lily, Rose, and Violet. Each garden has two kinds of flowers in it. In her garden, each twin has a flower with the same name as one of the other twins, not her own twin. Rose's garden has daisies, but Daisy's garden doesn't have roses. Heather grows ivy, and Ivy grows flowers that have the same name as Violet's twin sister, who is not Daisy. No two women whose names end in the letter "y" are sisters. Name the three sets of twins and the flowers they grow

READER'S JOURNAL

Choose a topic that relates to the readings in this unit, and write for about ten to twenty minutes. Consider using one of the quotes or one of the discussion questions in this unit as the basis for your writing.

READER'S JOURNAL

Date: _____

_____

_____

_____

_____

_____

_____

_____

_____

_____

_____

_____

_____

_____

_____

_____

_____

_____

_____

_____

_____

_____

_____

_____

_____

THERE'S NO PLACE LIKE HOME

FYi

Unit•3

Selections

In the English language, the words *house* and *home* have different connotations. A house is a building that functions as a place for people to live. While a home also is a place where people live, it connotes a place that evokes feelings of caring, comfort, and security. As you read the passages in this unit, you will notice several different attitudes toward *houses* and *homes*.

POINTS TO
PONDER

DISCUSSION

Think about and then discuss the following questions.

1. Where is your house?

2. Where is your home? If your answers to these questions are different, explain why.

3. What does the expression "Home is where the heart is" mean to you?

What's his thesis?

Gay Talese has had a long career in journalism as a correspondent for the *New York Times*. He is also the author of eight successful books. He is best known for *The Kingdom and the Power*, a history of the *New York Times*; *Honor Thy Father*, the story of a Mafia family; and *Thy Neighbor's Wife*, a book about the changing moral values in post–World War II America. Talese is considered one of the best nonfiction writers in America. An **essay** is a short piece of writing about a particular subject. In this "Coming Home" essay, Gay Talese talks about his definition of "home."

BEFORE YOU READ

FREEWRITING

When you think of the word *home*, what comes to mind? On a separate sheet of paper, freewrite for 10 minutes on the topic of *home*. Write as much as you can as fast as you can without worrying about mistakes.

● ●

Coming Home

To writer Gay Talese, home is a mood more than a particular address.

Gay Talese

Thesis

1   Home for me is a state of mind. When I'm feeling adventuresome and carefree, and perhaps confident, I think of New York City as my home. When I'm feeling reflective, private, and detached, I think of Ocean City, New Jersey.

2   I was born in 1932 in the aforementioned Ocean City, which is a Methodist community, founded by ministers. We were a minority within a minority—Italian Catholics in an Irish Catholic parish. My father, an immigrant, spoke English with an accent. I grew up feeling different, foreign, not part of America. That was my America—not being part of it.

3   Ocean City is a seashore resort; the industry was the sunshine, which brought the tourists from mid-June to Labor Day. But for those of us who lived there year round it was mainly without sunshine, cold and damp. It was an out-of-season place, and we were out-of-season people.

Facts to back up his thesis:
a) sometimes New York = his home
other times Ocean City = his home
b) U. 1 Alabama - new home to him   He often reads there
c) Par. 8 - although he grew up in Ocean City, remote apart

69

4   When I was seventeen I went away to the University of Alabama in Tuscaloosa, in the sunny Deep South. I felt like an explorer discovering a new America. Like Ocean City, it was a Protestant America, but it was friendly. In those days, of course, the university didn't have blacks; it had marginal whites—Jews, Greeks, Italians, and Lebanese. I was part of the Italian contingent.

5   The university was my salvation. I got a fresh start there, far away from gloomy Ocean City. No one knew of my bad grades, my reputation as a bad student, because no one knew me. Like an immigrant, I could abandon the past and start over. I took writing, and I thrived. Those were probably the happiest four years of my life.

6   I moved to New York in 1955 and have been here ever since. When I first moved here I read a novel called *The View from Pompey's Head*, by Hamilton Basso, which, if I recall it correctly, said that New York City is a city of neighborhoods in which no one has any neighbors. New York is not only a city without neighbors but one in which your sense of self is never very secure. It's also true that you can be yourself without anybody paying attention to you. The city is incredibly tolerant. You're part of something outrageously spectacular.

7   You do have to find your way into it. I think some of the points of entry might

be restaurants, familiar places where you see the same people—waiters, people who frequent the place. That's one reason I still go to Elaine's [restaurant] after thirty years.

8   Yet during my time in Alabama, and in the service and in my first decade in New York, I thought of Ocean City as a place I would someday like to return to. It represented writer's material. I bought a house there, not to integrate myself into the community—because I haven't; it's as remote to me now as when I was growing up—but as a setting from which to see the world. I measure much of what I write by Ocean City. I keep in mind always my sense of small-town America, old-fashioned values. It's a point of reference.

9   Still, the evidence strongly suggests that New York is where I should be; after all, I've been here 40 years. I've had the same phone number for four decades. I can't imagine living anyplace else. I have had opportunities to move and have chosen not to. But I don't have a sense of continuation and familiarity, which my daughters, who were born here, have. Maybe I write because I need to have something that can be familiar to me and it has to be language. Perhaps in putting down words I gain a sense of place.

conclusion

—by Catherine Sabino and Meakin Armstrong, USAir Magazine

A. **Read the following statements. If a statement is true according to Gay Talese, write *T* on the line. If it is false, write *F*. Then find the sentence in the article that supports the author's opinion, and write it on the lines provided.**

_____ 1. Ocean City is a beautiful place to live all during the year.

_____

_____

_____ 2. Tuscaloosa was similar to Ocean City in some ways.

_____

_____

_____ 3. New York is a city without neighbors, and your sense of self is not secure there.

_____

_____

_____ 4. Gay Talese feels closer to Ocean City as an adult than he did as a child.

_____

_____

_____ 5. Gay Talese bought a house in Ocean City in order to become a part of the community there.

_____

_____

_____ 6. Like his daughters, Gay Talese feels a sense of continuation and familiarity in New York City.

_____

_____

B. In "Coming Home," Gay Talese describes his impressions of both Ocean City and New York City. Write *OC* next to the phrases that describe Ocean City and *NYC* next to those that describe New York City.

_____ 1. a seashore resort

_____ 2. a tolerant city

_____ 3. usually cold and damp

_____ 4. a Methodist community

_____ 5. a city without neighbors

_____ 6. small-town America

_____ 7. old-fashioned values

_____ 8. an outrageously spectacular place

_____ 9. a gloomy place

_____ 10. a place where no one pays attention to you

RESPOND IN WRITING

1. In your own words, describe how Gay Talese felt when he was growing up in Ocean City.

   _____

   _____

   _____

2. In your own words, describe how Gay Talese felt when he went away to the University of Alabama.

   _____

   _____

   _____

EXPANDING VOCABULARY

Using a dictionary, write the part of speech for each word, the meaning as it is used in the article, any synonyms for the word, and a sentence to help you remember the meaning. For the last two items, choose words from the article that were unfamiliar to you.

1. salvation (¶5)

    part of speech: _____

    definition: _____

    synonyms: _____

    sentence: _____

    _____

2. gloomy (¶5)

    part of speech: _____

    definition: _____

    synonyms: _____

    sentence: _____

    _____

3. abandon (¶5)

    part of speech: _____

    definition: _____

    synonyms: _____

    sentence: _____

    _____

4. tolerant (¶6)

    part of speech: _____

    definition: _____

    synonyms: _____

    sentence: _____

    _____

5. spectacular (¶6)

   part of speech: _____

   definition: _____

   synonyms: _____

   sentence: _____

   _____

6. remote (¶8)

   part of speech: _____

   definition: _____

   synonyms: _____

   sentence: _____

   _____

7. _____ (¶   )

   part of speech: _____

   definition: _____

   synonyms: _____

   sentence: _____

   _____

8. _____ (¶   )

   part of speech: _____

   definition: _____

   synonyms: _____

   sentence: _____

   _____

Punctuation marks, such as dashes, can provide clues to help you understand the meaning of a sentence. Dashes may introduce examples, give an explanation, or indicate an abrupt shift in the thought of a sentence.

The following sentences from the article have dashes. Read the sentences and answer the questions.

1. *We were a minority within a minority—Italian Catholics in an Irish Catholic parish.*

   Why did Talese use a dash in this sentence?

   _____

2. *In those days, of course, the university didn't have blacks; it had marginal whites—Jews, Greeks, Italians, and Lebanese.*

   What are some examples of marginal whites?

   _____

3. *I think some of the points of entry might be restaurants, familiar places where you see the same people—waiters, people who frequent the place.*

   What are some examples of the same people?

   _____

4. *I bought a house there, not to integrate myself into the community—because I haven't; it's as remote to me now as when I was growing up—but as a setting from which to see the world.*

   Why did Talese put part of the sentence between dashes?

   _____

Richard Ford is the author of five novels and a collection of short stories. He won the 1996 Pulitzer Prize in literature for his novel *Independence Day*, a book that was subsequently made into a movie. Ford is known as one of America's greatest storytellers; he has said that working hard and gaining a large readership are more important to him than winning awards. As you read this "Coming Home" essay, think about what home means to Richard Ford.

BEFORE YOU READ

PREREADING DISCUSSION

1. Read the first sentence of the article. What do you think Ford means when he says "the mythical appeals and responsibilities and obligations of 'home'"?

2. Read the last sentence of the article. Do you agree that home is where someone loves you? Write your own short definition of home.

Home is _____

Coming Home

For Mississippi-raised novelist Richard Ford, home isn't a place, it's a state of mind.

Interview by Abigail Seymour

1   I have never invested one particular place with all of the mythical appeals and responsibilities and obligations of "home." My parents were from Arkansas, but because my father was a traveling salesman, they had lived more or less on the road. When my mother realized she was going to have a child, they thought they could settle in the middle of my father's territory, which covered seven states. They chose Mississippi for reasons of geographical convenience.

2   Home to me was the place where my father came home. My father was an extremely courtly, soft-spoken, large, sweet-natured man with a bit of a temper. He and I have that in common. He always wore brown suits and a tie, and I remember the soapy smell of his traveling kit. I think my mother cleaved to my father because she loved him, and because he was such a sweet and innocent man and she had not had a sweet nor innocent childhood.

She was a strong-willed person with a deep voice and hair that went gray early. They were mirthful people, both of them, and they liked to tell jokes. The fact that I was born was the embodiment of the greatest good luck to them.

3   My parents were first-generation urbanites who had come right off the farm. We ate good old Southern food in Jackson—fried chicken, salt pork, black-eyed peas. My favorite was lemon ice box pie with graham cracker crust. I remember waiting to eat watermelon in the backyard on the Fourth of July. In Mississippi in those days you still bought ice from a truck that would go up and down the street. You floated the watermelon whole with a big block of ice in one of those round, tin tubs with the two handles while you waited for it to cool.

4   Our house in Jackson was on Congress Street, right across from where Eudora Welty* had grown up. There was a slide in our backyard, and a spirea plant. We had wisteria, a magnolia tree, and holly. We lived next door to the Jefferson Davis school and summers were quite wonderful, because I was constantly reminded of what I was not doing. I remember going over to the school yard every day to play baseball with the kids from the neighborhood. We did a lot of swimming around there, too—Lake Pelahatchie, Livingston Lake, and later on we would sneak off and swim in the Pearl River. We even found an access to the enormous storm drains and used to make expeditions into the sewer system.

5   By the time I was old enough to walk around by myself, I noticed that most of the people in our neighborhood

Richard Ford

were quite elderly, and were not particularly congenial to a young kid they didn't know and whose family had moved from out of state, and whose father was mostly absent because he traveled. For me, adapting to my home became one of the principal predisposing habits to being a writer, because I was continually explaining myself, making my implausible presence plausible to adults.

6   Jackson was a place that was not that easy to break into, particularly at my parents' age. They didn't really know how to make friends, and people were suspicious of outsiders. It became simpler to just pack up the car and head back to Little Rock, which is what we did every Christmas. Part of my life was spent in a big hotel there, the Marion Hotel, which my grandparents managed. We went there, instead of to a house when we went to visit. I was always aware that they came from Arkansas.

* **Eudora Welty**   Early twentieth-century American author known for her stories about life in the rural southern United States.

7   I don't look for geography to give me refuge now. I've got several places where I'm really comfortable. I own a wonderful little house in Chinook, Montana, a town of 900 people. It's a farm and ranch community on the prairie right along U.S. Highway 2, which goes all the way from Maine to Washington. Chinook's got one clothing store, two newspapers, a big livestock auction barn, one pharmacy, two or three grain elevators, two car dealerships, four banks, and two grocery stores—one's an IGA and the other is Tom and Nancy's—where I shop, I'm very much at home there.

8   I also rent a big house in the Delta in Mississippi, and that's my home. My wife and I own a house on Bourbon Street in New Orleans, where she lives, and that's kind of a home, too. I'm probably one of the world's great adapters—it may be my only true skill. I don't need to be home to write. I write wherever I can stay and be quiet. I can suddenly make a home wherever I am in about an hour's time. Home now for me is not a place, it's a condition of mind. Home is where someone loves you.

HOW WELL DID YOU READ?

A. **Read the following statements. If a statement is true according to Richard Ford, write *T* on the line. If it is false, write *F*. Then find the sentence(s) in the article that supports the author's opinion, and write it on the lines provided.**

_____ 1. Ford's family moved to Mississippi because they had friends and family there.

_____

_____

_____ 2. Chinook, Montana is a small farming community.

_____

_____

_____ 3. The people of Jackson were friendly to newcomers.

_____

_____

_____ 4. Being adaptable is a skill that has helped Ford become a good writer.

_____

_____

B. Circle the letter of the choice that best answers the question.

1. In the second paragraph, Ford describes his parents. What word best describes the tone of the paragraph?

   a. humorous
   b. critical
   c. affectionate
   d. worried

2. In paragraph 3, Ford describes a memory from his childhood in Jackson. What emotion best describes his memory?

   a. nostalgia
   b. disgust
   c. unhappiness
   d. sympathy

3. In the final paragraph, Ford discusses his feelings about home and writing. What word best describes the tone of the paragraph?

   a. sarcastic
   b. pessimistic
   c. philosophical
   d. enthusiastic

EXPANDING VOCABULARY

Using a dictionary, write the part of speech for each word, the meaning as it is used in the article, any synonyms for the word, and a sentence to help you remember the meaning. For the last two items, choose words from the article that were unfamiliar to you.

1. convenience (¶1)

   part of speech: _____

   definition: _____

   synonyms: _____

   sentence: _____

   _____

2. mirthful (¶2)

   part of speech: _____

   definition: _____

   synonyms: _____

   sentence: _____

   _____

3. enormous (¶4)

part of speech: _____

definition: _____

synonyms: _____

sentence: _____

_____

4. congenial (¶5)

part of speech: _____

definition: _____

synonyms: _____

sentence: _____

_____

5. plausible (¶5)

part of speech: _____

definition: _____

synonyms: _____

sentence: _____

_____

6. refuge (¶7)

part of speech: _____

definition: _____

synonyms: _____

sentence: _____

_____

7. _____ (¶   )

part of speech: _____

definition: _____

synonyms: _____

sentence: _____

_____

8. —————— (¶   )

part of speech: _____

definition: _____

synonyms: _____

sentence: _____

_____

**RESPOND IN
WRITING**

A. **Reread the two essays, looking for comparisons between Gay Talese
   and Richard Ford. Make a list of three important similarities between
   the two men.**

1. _____

2. _____

3. _____

**Use your list as a guide to write a paragraph comparing Gay Talese and
Richard Ford.**

_____

_____

_____

_____

_____

_____

B. **Describe a memory from your own childhood.**

_____

_____

_____

_____

_____

_____

_____

Boston is the capital of and largest city in Massachusetts. It is located in the eastern part of the state at the mouth of the Charles River. Boston is one of the country's leading centers of culture, finance, and education. Many know it by one or more of its nicknames, "the cradle of liberty," "the hub of the solar system," and "the Athens of America," but to some it is also a place where people have no manners. Read "Does Boston Mind Its Manners?" to find out how well Boston compares with other cities in terms of politeness.

BEFORE YOU READ

PREREADING DISCUSSION

1. Do you think the people in your town or city have good manners? Why or why not? How do they usually treat outsiders or tourists?

2. What are some important rules of behavior in your culture?

3. Have you ever been to Boston? If so, did you like it? Did you find the people to be friendly? rude? helpful?

BEFORE YOU READ

PREREADING ACTIVITY

Get into groups with classmates from your part of the world. Make one list of behaviors that are considered good manners in your culture and another list of behaviors that are considered bad manners. Then compare and contrast your lists with those of the other groups.

Good Manners	**Bad Manners**
_____	_____
_____	_____
_____	_____
_____	_____
_____	_____
_____	_____
_____	_____
_____	_____
_____	_____

Does Boston Mind Its Manners?

B Y   S C O T   L E H I G H

GLOBE STAFF

Do you think Bostonians put out the welcome mat? Do you find other cities to be more—or less —polite?

1 Different cities have different feels for visitors. Some are friendly and open. Some are formal and distant.

2 Boston tends to seem hurried, and sometimes a little rude.

3 That's what some tourists have said.

4 One study found that people here are less willing to volunteer to help strangers than those residents of other U.S. cities.

5 Take a close look the next time you're in Boston, and here are some of the things you'll probably see:

• People smoking in the sub-way stations, despite the frequent reminders not to do so.

• Pedestrians walking when the crosswalk lights say not to do so, ignoring the cars.

• Car drivers speeding and honking and occasionally cursing at each other.

• Drivers who can't be bothered to find a place to park, but instead simply turn on their blinker and stop in the middle of the street.

6 Sometimes Bostonians seem like they're just too busy to be polite. Why is our city like that?

7 Former U.S. Rep. Chester Atkins says it's because the Puritan founding fathers were themselves impatient and grumpy and had little time for courtesy.

8 "We were founded of sourpusses, by sourpusses, for sourpusses," Atkins says. That culture has carried down to the present day, he believes.

Traffic and pedestrians in early twentieth century Boston.

9 Boston College professor Thomas O'Connor thinks a contributing factor is Boston's history as a city where each new group of immigrants was treated with suspicion and exclusion.

10 That's given Boston a sense of clannishness and reserve, he thinks. "The idea of a stranger greeting another stranger is simply not part of the local culture," he says. "People will begin a conversation with someone they know, but not with a stranger."

11 Ralph Whitehead, a professor of journalism at the University of Massachusetts at Amherst, thinks it's because Boston's upper class used manners to make class distinctions.

12 By being snobby about manners, Proper Bostonians made other people disdainful of courtesy, he says.

13 Some say that's just the way Boston is, and that the city will never change.

14 Still, other cities with reputations for worse rudeness are trying hard to change their images. Paris is one example where people are trying to be friendly. New York City is another. There, the city is trying to persuade subway riders to be more considerate.

15 If those cities can make the effort, maybe Boston should as well.

- -

HOW WELL DID YOU READ?

A. The author wonders why Bostonians often seem impolite. To answer this question, he summarizes the opinions of three Bostonians. In your own words, explain why each person thinks Boston is not a very polite city.

1. Chester Atkins: _____

   _____

2. Thomas O'Connor: _____

   _____

3. Ralph Whitehead: _____

   _____

B. Answer the questions.

1. What two cities does the author feel have worse reputations for rudeness than Boston?

   a. _____   b. _____

2. How are these cities trying to change their image?

   a. _____

   b. _____

3. What examples does the author give to support the point that "Boston tends to seem hurried, and sometimes a little rude"?

a. _____

b. _____

c. _____

d. _____

4. Based on the article and photograph, in what ways is the Boston of 100 years ago similar and different from the Boston of today?

a. _____

b. _____

c. _____

d. _____

EXPANDING VOCABULARY

Using a dictionary, write the part of speech for each word, the meaning as it is used in the article, any synonyms for the word, and a sentence to help you remember the meaning. For the last two items, choose words from the article that were unfamiliar to you.

1. pedestrian (¶5)

part of speech: _____

definition: _____

synonyms: _____

sentence: _____

_____

2. courtesy (¶7)

part of speech: _____

definition: _____

synonyms: _____

sentence: _____

_____

3. suspicion (¶9)

   part of speech: _____

   definition: _____

   synonyms: _____

   sentence: _____

   _____

4. exclusion (¶9)

   part of speech: _____

   definition: _____

   synonyms: _____

   sentence: _____

   _____

Tourism is the third largest industry in Massachusetts (after computers and investment banking). Few cities in the world can top the historical and cultural attractions of Boston.

5. disdainful (¶12)

   part of speech: _____

   definition: _____

   synonyms: _____

   sentence: _____

   _____

6. considerate (¶14)

   part of speech: _____

   definition: _____

   synonyms: _____

   sentence: _____

   _____

7. _____ (¶   )

part of speech: _____

definition: _____

synonyms: _____

sentence: _____

_____

8. _____ (¶   )

part of speech: _____

definition: _____

synonyms: _____

sentence: _____

_____

BUILDING READING SKILLS

INCREASING READING SPEED

You will have 20 seconds in which to underline the word that is the same as the first word in each line.

1. fish	shin	find	fine	fish	file
2. car	card	rock	car	care	rock
3. peach	reach	peach	pear	preach	peak
4. mint	money	mine	mime	mint	mink
5. all	ill	till	allot	I'll	all
6. shirt	shirk	trip	shirt	shin	stink
7. well	wells	swell	swelter	well	sweater
8. startle	starter	starting	started	startle	starts
9. heart	heat	art	heart	hear	healed
10. pants	pant	panther	stamp	pants	stomp
11. black	bleak	blend	black	block	blink
12. beef	bear	beef	bare	break	beat
13. lives	lived	lives	liver	liven	liken
14. union	onion	unit	units	union	reunion
15. radio	ratio	radiate	radon	radio	dacron

When you have finished, figure out how many answers you got right and check the appropriate box on page 263 in order to keep track of your progress.

RESPOND IN WRITING

Write a statement about the character of the city where you live or of another city that you are familiar with.

_____

Give four examples to prove your point.

1. _____

2. _____

3. _____

4. _____

Use your list to write a paragraph about the city you chose.

_____

_____

_____

_____

_____

_____

_____

_____

Read the following passage carefully. Then write an appropriate title. Compare your suggested title with those of your classmates. How are they alike and different? Do they focus on the same aspect of the article?

Feng Shui is the ancient Asian art of arranging one's environment, be it home or workplace, to achieve happiness and success. Invented more than 5,000 years ago in China, it has been practiced for centuries in many eastern cultures and is now gaining interest among Westerners as well.

Feng Shui is rooted in the basic principle that by balancing the earth's natural forces, we can tap into chi (good energy) and achieve harmony and good fortune. Masters of the art of Feng Shui are also called geomancers. They can measure a building's ability to attract good luck based on its design, shape, orientation, layout, and location. Because space so profoundly affects our sense of comfort and well-being, geomancers also advise clients on the placement of furniture and other objects as well as what colors, patterns, and textures to use in furnishings. Every building has its own harmony, and it is the role of the geomancer to bring good energy into the building and thus enhance the happiness and success of its inhabitants.

The message here is that if things are not going well, look at your environment. For example, if your back is to a door when you are sitting at your desk, you might want to rearrange your room. It's unsettling when you can't see who is coming through the door. Common sense also has a role in Feng Shui.[1]

The following story by Sandra Cisneros, "The House on Mango Street," describes the difference between the house the narrator's family dreamed about living in and the house that was their actual residence.

1. Where did you live when you were growing up? What was your house like? Describe it.

2. How did you feel about the house where you grew up? What did you like the most about it? The least? What words would you use to describe your attitude toward that house?

3. What memories do you have about growing up in that house?

Think about the house where you grew up. What comes to mind when you think about it? On a separate piece of paper, freewrite for ten minutes about that house. Write as much as you can as fast as you can without worrying about mistakes.

● ●

The House on Mango Street

BY SANDRA CISNEROS

1 We didn't always live on Mango Street. Before that we lived on Loomis on the third floor, and before that we lived on Keeler. Before Keeler it was Paulina, and before that I can't remember. But what I remember most is moving a lot. Each time it seemed there'd be one more of us. By the time we got to Mango Street we were six—Mama, Papa, Carlos, Kiki, my sister Nenny and me.

2 The house on Mango Street is ours, and we don't have to pay rent to anybody, or share the yard with the people downstairs, or be careful not to make too much noise, and there isn't a landlord banging on the ceiling with a broom. But even so, it's not the house we'd thought we'd get.

3 We had to leave the flat on Loomis quick. The water pipes broke and the landlord wouldn't fix them because the house was too old. We had to leave

fast. We were using the washroom next door and carrying water over in empty milk gallons. That's why Mama and Papa looked for a house, and that's why we moved into the house on Mango Street, far away, on the other side of town.

negative details

4   They always told us that one day we would move into a house, a real house that would be ours for always so we wouldn't have to move each year. And our house would have running water and pipes that worked. And inside it would have real stairs, not hallway stairs, but stairs inside like the houses on T.V. And we'd have a basement and at least three washrooms so when we took a bath we wouldn't have to tell everybody. Our house would be white with trees around it, a great big yard and grass growing without a fence. This was the house Papa talked about when he held a lottery ticket and this was the house Mama dreamed up in the stories she told us before we went to bed.

5   But the house on Mango Street is not the way they told it at all. It's small and red with tight steps in front and windows so small you'd think they were holding their breath. Bricks are crumbling in places, and the front door is so swollen you have to push hard to get in. There is no front yard, only four little elms the city planted by the curb. Out back is a small garage for the car we don't own yet and a small yard that looks smaller between the two buildings on either side. There are stairs in our house, but they're ordinary hallway stairs, and the house has only one washroom. Everybody has to share a bedroom—Mama and Papa, Carlos and Kiki, me and Nenny.

6   Once when we were living on Loomis, a nun from my school passed by and saw me playing out front. The laundromat downstairs had been boarded up because it had been robbed two days before and the owner had painted on the wood YES WE'RE OPEN so as not to lose business.

7   Where do you live? she asked.

8   There, I said pointing up to the third floor.

9   You live *there*?

10   *There.* I had to look to where she pointed—the third floor, the paint peeling, wooden bars Papa had nailed on the windows so we wouldn't fall out. You live *there*? The way she said it made me feel like nothing. *There.* I lived *there*, I nodded.

11   I knew then I had to have a house. A real house. One I could point to. But this isn't it. The house on Mango Street isn't it. For the time being, Mama says. Temporary, says Papa. But I know how those things go.

● ●

Circle the letter of the choice that best completes the sentence or answers the question.

1. The author describes the house on Mango Street with a tone of _____.

   a. disappointment
   b. joy
   c. pride
   d. humor

2. Cisneros mentions _____ .

   a. one other place where her family lived
   b. several other places where her family lived
   c. where her grandparents live
   d. where her family plans to move

3. Cisneros's family had to move from Loomis Street because _____ .

   a. they couldn't pay the rent
   b. their house was robbed
   c. the water pipes broke
   d. they won the lottery

4. In describing the house on Mango Street, which of the following does the author not mention?

   a. the kitchen
   b. the stairs
   c. the windows
   d. the front door

5. The word *them* in paragraph 3 refers to _____ .

   a. the landlord
   b. the milk gallons
   c. the Cisneros family
   d. the water pipes

6. The word *ordinary* in paragraph 5 is closest in meaning to which of the following?

   a. small
   b. common
   c. tight
   d. old

**BUILDING
READING SKILLS**

MAKING
INFERENCES

An **inference** is a reasonable conclusion that you make based on information provided in the text. It is an educated guess. Inferences are not stated directly, but good readers try to make inferences using information implied in the text and clues provided by the writer.

Check the inferences you can logically make from *The House on Mango Street*.

_P. 2_   1. The family didn't like to move from place to place.

_P. 3_   2. Sandra was ashamed of the place where she lived on Loomis Street.

_P. 11_ 3. Sandra doesn't believe that the house on Mango Street is temporary.

_P. 6_   4. The owner of the laundromat lived in the same building as Sandra's family.

_no_   5. Sandra's family eventually moved to a white house with trees and a back yard.

_no_   6. Sandra's parents enjoy lying to their children.

_____   7. Sandra's family didn't have a lot of money.

**RESPOND IN
WRITING**

Reread the description of the house on Mango Street in paragraph 5. What details does Cisneros use to describe the house?

_____

_____

_____

_____

_____

_____

Now think about the place where you live. Make a list of descriptive details about the place.

_____

_____

_____

_____

_____

_____

Use your list to write a description of the place where you live on a separate piece of paper.

Many people have strong feelings about the house they grew up in. Sandra Cisneros felt that her house on Mango Street was like a prison. Now read the following essay in which a young boy describes his fond feelings for the house he is about to leave.

My House

BY DANIEL LOURIE

1   My mother moved a lot when she was growing up. Her family never stayed in any one place more than a year or so, on account of Grandpa being in the army. She hated those years of moving all the time, having to adjust to new schools and make new friends. That's why I thought she was joking when she sprang the idea of moving on me. But for once in her life she wasn't joking. This time she was completely serious. My mother has decided that this house is too big for just the two of us and that an apartment in the city would suit our needs much better. Personally, I think she's lost her mind. I guess I can understand why she would want to move, but what about me and what this house means to me?

2   I suppose if you looked at my house, you might think it was just another suburban colonial, housing just another Elkington family. But let me assure you, this sturdy house that has been my home for ten years is anything but standard. My father, my mother, and I moved into this house when I was three years old. I can still remember that first day in our new house like it was yesterday. The first thing I noticed was the big front yard. To me it seemed like an ocean of grass—I couldn't wait to dive in. The backyard was full of trees, the gnarled and scary kind that talk at night when the wind blows. But as time went by, I grew to like the trees and the shadows they cast in my room. My father and I built a small tree house in one of the bigger trees. It's still a place I like to go to remember my father and all the wonderful times we had before he died.

3   This house is special—maybe only to me—but special nevertheless. The idea of living in any other house seems absurd. Opening any other front door, looking out any other windows just wouldn't feel like home. It's the little, seemingly insignificant things, that make this house so special to me: the ice-cold tile floors that make me shiver on midnight snack runs; the paint that creeps away from the molding revealing a rainbow of colors that had peeled, been forgotten, then painted over; the smell of my father's pipe that still lingers in the walls; the towering built-in bookcases that hold my mother's personal library of trashy romance novels and "get-rich-quick" books; the view out my bedroom window.

4   It's not true that we can simply move and make another house our home. This house has been my refuge, my castle. It holds too many important memories, memories that would be lost if we gave it up.[2]

RESPOND IN WRITING

Think about the differences between the feelings Sandra Cisneros and Daniel Lourie have about the houses they grew up in. How do you feel about the place where you grew up? Write an essay describing your memories and feelings about that place.

_____

_____

_____

_____

_____

_____

_____

_____

_____

_____

_____

_____

_____

_____

_____

_____

_____

_____

_____

_____

_____

_____

_____

_____

_____

_____

FYi

The total number of housing units in the United States is 103,253,000. Fifty-nine percent of them are owner-occupied.

TALK IT OVER

DISCUSSION

Edgar Guest is a British author who is known for his poetry about friendship and family life. He has said, "It takes a lot of living in a house to make it a home."[3] How do you think Sandra Cisneros would react to his statement?

1. Now that you have finished the readings in this unit, do you want to change your answers to Points to Ponder questions 1 and 2: Where is your house? Where is your home? If you decide to change your answers, what would you change them to?

2. In light of your reading in this unit, discuss the English expression "A house is not a home."

3. Thomas Wolfe (1900–1938) wrote a book entitled *You Can't Go Home Again.* Do you agree that you can go back to your former house but not to your former home?

4. The artist Andy Warhol (1928–1987) said, "My ideal city would be one long Main Street with no cross streets or side streets to jam up traffic. Just one big, long street."[4] What would your ideal city look like?

5. "Every city has a sex and an age which have nothing to do with demography. Rome is feminine. So is Odessa. London is a teenager, an urchin, and in this it hasn't changed since the time of Charles Dickens. Paris, I believe, is a man in his twenties in love with an older woman."[5] How would you characterize your city and other cities you know?

6. The German novelist and poet Hermann Hesse (1877–1962) wrote, "One never reaches home, but wherever friendly paths intersect, the whole world looks like home for a time."[6] Do you agree or disagree with this statement?

7. Primo Levi (1919–1987) was an Italian chemist and author. He said, "I live in my house as I live inside my skin: I know more beautiful, more ample, more sturdy and more picturesque skins: but it would seem to me unnatural to exchange them for mine."[7] Do you feel like that about your house?

Look at the drawing on the previous page and try to remember as much of it as you can. Study the drawing below and do the same. Then cover both drawings and use the spaces to list all the differences between the two pictures that you can remember.

_____

_____

_____

_____

_____

_____

_____

_____

Check your answers in the Answer Key on page 264.

READER'S
JOURNAL

Choose a topic that relates to the readings in this unit and write for about ten to twenty minutes. Consider using one of the quotes or one of the discussion questions in this unit as the basis for your writing.

READER'S JOURNAL

Date: _____

_____

_____

_____

_____

_____

_____

_____

_____

_____

_____

_____

_____

_____

_____

_____

_____

_____

_____

_____

_____

_____

_____

_____

_____

_____

_____

_____

ATHLETES **A**ND **R**OLE **M**ODELS

FYi

Unit·4

Selections

The subject of sports is one that comes up frequently in casual conversation and in the news. It is a topic that almost everyone knows something about. This unit looks at several much-discussed topics relating to sports, including athletes as role models and the relevance of the modern Olympic Games.

POINTS TO
PONDER

DISCUSSION

Think about and then discuss the following questions.

1. What sports do you like to watch, play, read or talk about?

2. Who do you consider to be the best athletes in those sports?

3. In your native country, are athletes celebrities? Do they make enormous salaries and get lucrative advertising contracts?

4. Freewrite for ten minutes on the topic of sports.

_____

_____

_____

_____

_____

_____

_____

_____

_____

_____

_____

_____

_____

_____

_____

_____

Athletes are often viewed as role models because they accomplish feats many of us cannot. As you will read in the article "Athletes as Role Models," they also tend to demonstrate positive traits such as dedication and self-control, qualities anyone can emulate.

BEFORE YOU READ

PREREADING ACTIVITY

In column A make a list of athletes you can think of throughout history who have been important in the world of sports. In column B indicate their sports. Compare your list with that of your classmates.

A   B

_____   _____

_____   _____

_____   _____

_____   _____

_____   _____

_____   _____

_____   _____

_____   _____

_____   _____

BUILDING READING SKILLS

PREVIEWING

Before you read the article, spend a few minutes previewing it by completing the following steps.

1. Read the title. Think about what it means and try to predict what the general topic of the article might be.

2. Read the headings that are written in bold print. How do you think the author will develop the topic? Try to anticipate the kind of information that might be included in each section of the article.

3. Read the first and last paragraphs. What technique does the author use to introduce the topic in the first paragraph? What conclusion does she make in the last paragraph?

4. Read the first sentence of each paragraph, and think about how the article is organized and how the topic is developed.

5. Make a list of points you think the author might discuss in the article.

_____

_____

_____

_____

_____

Athletes as Role Models

By Sheila Globus

1   Everyone loves sports stars. They look great, they appear on television, and like rock stars, they perform with the entire world watching. No wonder we make heroes out of our favorites. Great athletes teach us more than how to swing a bat or block a pass. In the face of seemingly impossible challenges, they teach us that success—whether on the basketball court or in the classroom—takes dedication, confidence, and a hefty dose of hard work.

Sports Stars Are People, Too

2   Athletes are seen as heroes because they can do things that most of us can't do. They can hit fastballs coming at them at nearly 100 miles an hour, and leap and hang in the air, seemingly defying gravity, or slam a ball over a net. They get paid millions of dollars for their efforts, and their names and faces appear on everything from running shoes to billboards. Their words are repeated and broadcast around the world.

3   Athletes who are champions also show qualities such as perseverance, dedication, and the ability to keep their cool under pressure. Many show those same qualities off the playing field, too. Stories about superstar athletes teach us about working hard and believing in ourself and in being passionate about what we do. Although it's usually bad behavior that gets an athlete a spot on the six o'clock news, many high-profile players work hard to be positive role models to children. They raise money for charities and act

as mentors, talking to student groups and volunteering their time to programs that help kids stay off drugs and stay in school.

4   Still, even the greatest champions have flaws. Just because an athlete has the perfect golf swing doesn't mean he or she is the perfect parent, friend, or spokesperson. Even rich, famous, and successful people get sick and face the same problems other people do.

Sammy Sosa

They also make mistakes. Separating an athlete's professional and personal life can be tough. When a sports star gets in trouble with the law, or does something wrong in his or her private life, fans are often left disappointed. Before he died, baseball great Mickey Mantle, who was plagued with alcohol problems, told young ball players and the fans who idolized and admired him to "play like me; don't be like me."

Against All Odds

5   Some sports heroes have overcome daunting obstacles to rise to the top of their sport. In 1947, for example, Jackie Robinson of the Brooklyn Dodgers became the first African-American to play in the modern major leagues. Former Olympian Wilma Rudolph was born with polio and survived pneumonia and scarlet fever as a child. All these ailments left her with a bad leg that some said would

prevent her even from walking. Although she wore a leg brace from the time she was 5 until she was 11, Rudolph still managed to play basketball and go out for track when she was 13. While still a high school sophomore, she competed in the 1956 Olympic Games. These days, Rudolph is remembered for her inspirational determination to overcome her physical challenges, and for her courage in rising above segregation and racism.

6   More recently, hockey star Mario Lemieux showed similar courage when he was diagnosed with cancer. Statistics show him to be one of this era's greatest hockey players, in spite of the many games he was forced to miss due to his illness.

Keeping Things in Perspective

7   Courage and determination aren't the only lessons we can learn from successful athletes. Some of the greatest sports figures, past and present, are those who can take their athletic achievements in stride. You have to love a sport to do it and to do it well. But you also have to know how not to get caught up in the glory and the hype, especially when the crowds are cheering for somebody else.

8   Hard-working and highly motivated athletes understand that there is more to sports than winning. Being the top

scorer or having the best batting average or the fastest time are less important than just giving it your best shot, whatever the outcome. Champion distance runner Joan Benoit Samuelson says it best: "Winning is neither everything nor the only thing. It is one of many things."

Practice Makes Perfect

9 Top athletes are constantly striving to improve. What's more, they can stay focused, often under intense pressure. (Who can forget gymnast Kerri Strug's stunning vault, despite an injured leg, that sent her team to a gold-medal finish at the 1996 Olympic Games?) You don't need to be in the Olympics to be a team player and be committed to what you're doing. It's fine to admire Michael Jordan's wizardry on the basketball court or Picabo Street's finesse on the ski slopes. To rise to the top of any profession or sport, though, takes countless hours of practice to fine-tune the skills needed to accomplish your goals.

The Power of Positive Thinking

10 Ever wonder how Michael Jordan can sink a foul shot in front of thousands of people waving their arms and shouting, and not get distracted? Great athletes can focus their total concentration on the task at hand. They also arrive at the field, rink, or pool feeling like a winner. They visualize winning and tackle each game or event with spirit and determination. Overconfident? Not really. How often does the team rated the underdog win the game? Just look at the World Series champion Florida Marlins.

Being Your Best

11 Star athletes learn from their mistakes as well as from their successes. They have what it takes to be a winner. Remember that qualities like fairness, sportsmanship, honesty, and determination also can be found in everyday people—your teachers, a coach at school, and your parents.

HOW WELL DID YOU READ?

Answer the questions in complete sentences.

1. According to the article, what is the most important thing that sports heroes teach us?

_____

_____

2. Why are athletes often seen as heroes?

_____

_____

3. What are some things that high-profile players do to be positive role models to children?

_____

_____

4. Why did baseball superstar Mickey Mantle tell his fans to "play like me; don't be like me"?

_____

_____

5. What obstacles did each of the following athletes have to overcome to achieve success?
   a. Jackie Robinson

   _____

   _____

   b. Wilma Rudolph

   _____

   _____

   c. Mario Lemieux

   _____

   _____

6. What do highly motivated top athletes understand about winning?

_____

_____

7. What does it take to rise to the top and accomplish your goals?

_____

_____

8. According to the article, what qualities does it take to be a winner?

_____

_____

BUILDING READING SKILLS

UNDERSTANDING POINT OF VIEW

Put a check mark next to the statements you think the author would agree with.

——— 1. Being the best and winning are the most important aspects of sports.

——— 2. To be at the top of any profession or sport takes a commitment to practice and hard work.

——— 3. Great athletes teach us more than just the skill of their sport.

——— 4. All great champions are perfect.

——— 5. Underdogs often win because they are determined and focused.

——— 6. You don't have to be a star athlete to be a winner.

——— 7. It's impossible not to get caught up in the glory when you're a sports star.

BUILDING WRITING SKILLS

SUMMARIZING

Write a one-paragraph summary of the important points of the article.

_____

_____

_____

_____

_____

_____

_____

RESPOND IN WRITING

In your opinion, what makes someone a good role model?

_____

_____

_____

_____

_____

_____

EXPANDING VOCABULARY

Using a dictionary, write the part of speech for each word, the meaning as it is used in the article, any synonyms for the word, and a sentence to help you remember the meaning. For the last three items, choose words from the article that were unfamiliar to you.

1. perseverance (¶3)

   part of speech: _____

   definition: _____

   synonyms: _____

   sentence: _____

   _____

2. mentor (¶3)

   part of speech: _____

   definition: _____

   synonyms: _____

   sentence: _____

   _____

3. flaw (¶4)

   part of speech: _____

   definition: _____

   synonyms: _____

   sentence: _____

   _____

4. idolize (¶4)

   part of speech: _____

   definition: _____

   synonyms: _____

   sentence: _____

   _____

5. obstacle (¶5)

   part of speech: _____

   definition: _____

   synonyms: _____

   sentence: _____

   _____

6. strive (¶9)

   part of speech: _____

   definition: _____

   synonyms: _____

   sentence: _____

   _____

7. determination (¶11)

   part of speech: _____

   definition: _____

   synonyms: _____

   sentence: _____

   _____

8. _____ (¶   )

   part of speech: _____

   definition: _____

   synonyms: _____

   sentence: _____

   _____

9. _____ (¶   )

   part of speech: _____

   definition: _____

   synonyms: _____

   sentence: _____

   _____

10. _____ (¶   )

   part of speech: _____

   definition: _____

   synonyms: _____

   sentence: _____

   _____

SELECTION 2

There was public condemnation and outrage when basketball superstar Charles Barkley declared in an athletic shoe commercial, "I'm not paid to be a role model." The exploits of Michael Jordan and Charles Barkley have stirred a debate about just what pro athletes owe their fans. The article that follows, "I'm Not a Role Model," explores both sides of this issue.

BEFORE YOU READ

PREREADING DISCUSSION

1. What personal qualities do you think make someone a good role model?

2. Do you believe that athletes have a responsibility to act as role models to their fans?

I'm Not a Role Model

1   It's hard to believe now, but there was, supposedly, a time when every pink-faced, pug-nosed American youngster wanted more than anything to grow up to be president. Well, as any casual visit to the haunts of the young and unfamous will show, the aspirations of youth have undergone a change. If kids can be said to vote with their T-shirts these days, it's sports stardom over politics by a landslide. Across the country, from West Hollywood to Miami Beach, mall rats are flaunting the leaping likenesses of Michael Jordan and Charles Barkley on their chests. Presidents can raise taxes and wage war; but did Bill Clinton—or Hillary—ever pump in 55 points in a playoff game?

2   Accordingly, the revelation that the slam-dunking Jordan has been running up scores in Atlantic City casinos, too, has rekindled some sharp debate about the obligation of sports figures to set examples for the young. In the brusquely forthright words of Barkley: "I'm not paid to be a role model, I'm paid to wreak havoc on the basketball court." That observation, immortalized in a widely seen television commercial, has stirred up roughly equal measures of support and dissent. "In essence Barkley is correct." says Boston College sociologist Michael Malec, former editor of the *Journal of Sport and Social Issues*. "If you want to emulate what he does on court, you've got a wonderful model there. That doesn't necessarily mean he ought to be a model as a father or husband." But others saw the remark as merely rationalizing Barkley's own

uncourtly deportment. "Funny, how big shots accept all the trappings of role modeldom—especially the residual commercial cash—*before* they renounce their broader responsibilities to society," scolded *New York Post* sports watchdog Phil Mushnick. And fellow hoopster Karl Malone, in a column written for *Sports Illustrated*, chided Barkley directly: "Charles . . . I don't think it's your decision to make. We don't *choose* to be role models, we are *chosen*. Our only choice is whether to be a good role model or a bad one."

3   The debate itself has undergone a transformation; the Pollyanna premises of old have given way to the latter-day realpolitik of tarnished celebrity.* Says sociologist Charles Payne, professor of African-American and urban studies at Northwestern University: "If you were to go through baseball's or football's Hall of Fame, you're not going to come up with a bunch of choirboys." Most fans, in any case, seem perfectly willing to overlook Jordan's gambling caper. For one thing, unlike Pete Rose, he hasn't been reckless enough to bet on his own sport. "It was just something he did for fun, not anything to harm anything," says 12-year-old Genny Sonday, of Lincoln, Neb., speaking for many of her peers.

4   But that doesn't quite get the ball jocks off the hook. Celebrities like Barkley may decline the honor, but their high visibility obliges them to behave with at least an awareness that they are being watched by millions. Like it or not, they have a power of influence on worshipful young fans multiplied by the huge factor of television—perhaps even more so among the minority poor, who have few other

*In other words, celebrities are no longer expected to be perfect.

avatars of success to excite their hopes. It may be well and good to point out, as most child psychologists do, that parents are the main role models in a child's life. But that smugly assumes an intact and caring set of parents to do the job. "What does it say to the kid who doesn't really have anybody?" asks Dr. Robert Burton, a Northwestern University psychiatrist who specializes in treating athletes. "Kids need to have someone they can idealize in order to aspire to become better themselves. Without that, there's not much hope for them."

> **Charles, you can deny being a role model all you want, but I don't think it's your decision to make. We don't choose to be role models, we are chosen. Our only choice is whether to be a good role model or a bad one.**
>
> **Karl Malone, Utah Jazz**

5   Role models operate on more than one level. Parents and teachers are the guiding lights for everyday reality. Star athletes and other celebrities—the Muhammad Alis and Babe Ruths, the Jordans and Barkleys—are the models in daydreams. They represent an impossible dream, perhaps, but something to grow on. Yet as press coverage of sports becomes less and less worshipful, these fantasy figures begin to look less than ideal. "They're womanizers, they're gamblers . . . they spit," says Carol Lorente, a Bolingbrook, Ill., magazine editor who has conflicting feelings about her 9-year-old son Paul's dreams of becoming a major-league player. "I don't expect my son to do those things

because he's heard they do them. On the other hand, he wants to be one of those guys." In fact, there's little evidence in social-science literature that children actually adopt the behavior of athletes they adore. When Michael Jordan began wearing long shorts, young basketball enthusiasts everywhere suddenly began turning up in the knee-length look. But that doesn't mean they will model their lives on Jordan's. "There are not going to be many who say, 'Well, Michael Jordan gambles, then I'm gonna gamble,'" says Gary Alan Fine, head of the sociology department at the University of Georgia and author of a book on Little League baseball.

6   On the whole, says Fine, celebrity role models no longer have such a huge impact on children, most of whom are fairly sophisticated by the time they reach the pre-adolescent years. "They don't have these wide-eyed beliefs that sports figures are somehow superhuman." Often, it's the parents, more than their children, who wind up being disillusioned. Dr. Gerald Dabbs, spokesman for the New York Council for Child Psychiatry, remembers that when Pee-Wee Herman was arrested for indecent exposure in a movie theater a few years ago, not a single child brought it up with him, but the parents did. Parents can set the tone for a child's response to models. "Forgiveness can also be part of role modeling," he says, "and understanding that people the children admire can do things that are disappointing, or even wrong." In fact, says Dabbs, there's nothing wrong with the dose of reality the kids get when a sports hero stumbles, although older children are likely to absorb it more easily, "When good people do bad things,

part of what they get from that is learning to come to terms with one's own limitations," he says.

7 **Mesmerizing focus:** Television, with its ability to move in close and parse the action, has certainly brought the skills of players like Jordan into mesmerizing focus. But in spite of the tube, or perhaps because of it, celebrity heroes now appear to be more fleeting and fragmented, like the culture they come out of. Janet Harris, a professor in the department of physical education at the University of North Carolina, asked children and adolescents whom they most want to be like. "They had a lot of trouble answering," she says. "Most identified no one person, but several people with different characteristics. We ended up not even using the data." As part of her study, to be released in her forthcoming book, "Athletes and the American Hero Dilemma," Harris analyzed popularity lists published in the World Almanac and found most of those selected remained on the list only a year or two. (Jordan, an exception, hung in for six, until the last time the list was published.) When a star stumbles, it's so widely and avidly reported now that even the very young can hardly avoid hearing about it. But the University of Georgia's Fine, for one, believes that such exposure gives kids a more accurate idea of adults and society in general. "This is what adults are," says Fine. "One of the things kids have to learn is to make decisions about what the world is like and then make decisions on how to fit into that world." That's a lesson some of our more refractory superstars might do well to ponder, too.

_____

David Gelman with Karen Springen in Chicago and Sudarsan Raghavan in Los Angeles

HOW WELL DID YOU READ?

Read the following statements. If a statement is true, write *T* on the line. If it is false, write *F*.

_____ 1. Most American children today want to grow up to be president.

_____ 2. Basketball superstar Charles Barkley wants to be a role model.

_____ 3. The author of the article believes that sports celebrities should behave with an awareness that they are being watched by millions.

_____ 4. According to the article, role models operate on more than one level.

_____ 5. The evidence in social science literature strongly supports the idea that children adopt the behavior of their favorite athletes.

_____ 6. Many children and adolescents have a hard time choosing one person they most want to be like.

_____ 7. Children think sports figures are superhuman.

**BUILDING
WRITING SKILLS**

PARAPHRASING

Rewrite the sentences below using your own words. Your sentences should express the main idea of the original sentences as clearly and simply as possible.

1. *[A]s any casual visit to the haunts of the young and unfamous will show, the aspirations of youth have undergone a change. If kids can be said to vote with their T-shirts these days, it's sports stardom over politics by a landslide.*

_____

_____

_____

_____

2. *It may be well and good to point out, as most child psychologists do, that parents are the main role models in a child's life. But that smugly assumes an intact and caring set of parents to do the job.*

_____

_____

_____

_____

3. *On the whole, says Fine, celebrity role models no longer have such a huge impact on children, most of whom are fairly sophisticated by the time they reach the pre-adolescent years.*

_____

_____

_____

_____

4. *Television, with its ability to move in close and parse the action, has certainly brought the skills of players like Jordan into mesmerizing focus. But in spite of the tube, or perhaps because of it, celebrity heroes now appear to be more fleeting and fragmented, like the culture they come out of.*

_____

_____

_____

_____

RESPOND IN WRITING

Write a paragraph explaining whether you agree or disagree with this state-ment: *Star athletes have a responsibility to serve as role models.*

_____

_____

_____

_____

_____

_____

_____

EXPANDING VOCABULARY

Using a dictionary, write the part of speech for each word, the meaning as it is used in the article, any synonyms for the word, and a sentence to help you remember the meaning. For the last three items, choose words from the article that were unfamiliar to you.

1. aspiration (¶1)

   part of speech: _____

   definition: _____

   synonyms: _____

   sentence: _____

   _____

2. revelation (¶2)

   part of speech: _____

   definition: _____

   synonyms: _____

   sentence: _____

   _____

3. dissent (¶2)

   part of speech: _____

   definition: _____

   synonyms: _____

   sentence: _____

   _____

4. emulate (¶2)

part of speech: _____

definition: _____

synonyms: _____

sentence: _____

_____

5. deportment (¶2)

part of speech: _____

definition: _____

synonyms: _____

sentence: _____

_____

6. renounce (¶2)

part of speech: _____

definition: _____

synonyms: _____

sentence: _____

_____

7. transformation (¶3)

part of speech: _____

definition: _____

synonyms: _____

sentence: _____

_____

8. reckless (¶3)

part of speech: _____

definition: _____

synonyms: _____

sentence: _____

_____

9. aspire (¶4)

part of speech: _____

definition: _____

synonyms: _____

sentence: _____

_____

10. fleeting (¶7)

part of speech: _____

definition: _____

synonyms: _____

sentence: _____

_____

11. _____ (¶   )

part of speech: _____

definition: _____

synonyms: _____

sentence: _____

_____

12. _____ (¶   )

part of speech: _____

definition: _____

synonyms: _____

sentence: _____

_____

13. _____ (¶   )

part of speech: _____

definition: _____

synonyms: _____

sentence: _____

_____

The Olympic Games have endured a stormy history. They originated in Greece in 776 B.C. At that time people believed that athletic competition pleased the spirits of the gods. As time went on, the games lost their religious meaning and the athletes became interested only in winning money. For this reason, in A.D. 394 Emperor Theodosius ended the Olympic Games. In 1875 Baron Pierre de Coubertin revived them. He believed that athletics could play an important part in promoting world peace. Despite recent scandals involving a few athletes and the choosing of Olympic sites by administrators of the Olympic Games, it appears that the baron's foresight is justified.

"Warning: Games Seriously Damage Health" is an example of an *editorial*. An editorial is a piece of writing in a newspaper or magazine that gives the opinion of the writer rather than reporting facts. As you read this editorial, think about whether or not you agree with the author's opinions.

BEFORE YOU READ

PREREADING DISCUSSION

1. Do you like to watch the Olympic Games on TV? Have you ever attended them in person? Did you aspire to being an Olympic athlete when you were younger? If yes, in what sport? How old were you?

2. Do you agree with Pierre de Coubertin that athletics could play an important part in promoting world peace? In what ways? Do you think they do play such a role? Explain why or why not.

● ●

Warning: Games Seriously Damage Health

Olympic athletes are doubtful role models for average citizen.

"If you are healthy you don't need it; if you are sick you shouldn't take it."
—Henry Ford* on exercise

[1] Those who deplore the blatant commercialism of the modern Olympic Games and reminisce about the days when real amateurs competed just for the joy of taking part have overlooked the history of athletic sports. In ancient Greece, an athlete was one who contended for a prize in musical, equestrian, gymnastic, or any other competitions. The name subsequently became restricted to competitors in gymnastic contests and later to the class of professional athletes. By the 5th century B.C. the largely upper-class males who competed for

* Henry Ford developed the gasoline-powered car and founded the Ford Motor Company in 1903.

the glory alone had been usurped by those from the lower orders who took up athletics to earn a living. Disdainfully, the men of superior birth refused to associate with their inferiors, yet remained sufficiently interested to become spectators. And those latter-day couch potatoes certainly had plenty to watch as naked male athletes, bodies gleaming with oily salve, ran, threw the discus, boxed, and wrestled (the highest achievement).

2   As for the athletes themselves, they underwent rigorous training. Nothing like bending an iron rod or taming a bull to keep you fit, all fortified by the prescribed diet of fresh cheese, dried figs, and wheaten bread. An athlete could start his career as a boy in age-restricted contests, and continue to appear as a youth and as an adult, being debarred at age 35. None of this found favor with ancient philosophers, moralists, and physicians, who almost to a man roundly condemned the profession of athletics as being injurious to both mind and body.

3   So what has changed? Women; clothes, which become briefer every year and would probably be skimpier still if that did not preclude a manufacturer's logo; more events (rhythmic gymnastics, synchronized swimming, and beach volleyball have all been on offer at recent Olympic Games); and computerized scoring systems with a level of accuracy that would probably cost an ancient Greek scribe his life. And the marvel of telecommunications brings every last drop of sweat into homes across the globe, where people with no ostensible sporting inclinations still find themselves glued to the television screen.

4   Those who promote exercise as a way to keep healthy use an Olympic year to urge slothful individuals to engage in physical activity; a recently released report from the U.S. Surgeon General's Office is one example. But we believe the Olympic Games are giving sensible exercise a bad name. There are athletes in Atlanta who have grappled with all manner of injuries acquired in the course of their chosen career; one hears of surgery to overcome damage to runners' knees and ankles, hurdlers' groins, and javelin throwers' shoulders, so that individuals can reach the pinnacle of their profession. The pressures lead some to take performance-enhancing drugs. There are athletes who collapse in agony while competing, and those who struggle on "heroically." Many have no semblance of a normal family life for years, placing themselves and those around them under immense strain. Are these really ideal role models, let alone good examples for exercise of a less damaging nature?

5   What about the athletes? Many top-class competitors will be lucky to escape severe osteoarthritis as a long-term consequence of serious injury; for women, the effects of exercise-induced amenorrhea can seriously affect bone mass. Who knows what the contorsions of young gymnasts are doing to their spines; raising of the competitive age for females from 15 to 16 (in the year of competition) after the 1996 Games must signify some concern by the sport's governing body. And if they do not get to the top, sports men and women are discarded more speedily than the average racing greyhound.

6   Although the semi-professional modern Olympics may be closer to the origins of athletics than most people realize, the Games have become a tawdry spectacle and a serious threat to competitors' health. Health promoters who jump on the Olympic bandwagon to extol the virtues of exercise to the general public should think again.

conclusion

● ●

HOW WELL DID YOU READ?

Circle the letter of the choice that best completes the sentence or answers the question.

1. The author's tone in this editorial is _____ .

   a. sympathetic
   b. humorous
   c. critical
   d. hesitant

2. The author's main point is that the _____ .

   a. original Olympic athletes underwent rigorous training
   b. Olympic games pose a serious threat to competitors' health
   c. modern Olympics are very different from their ancient Greek counterpart
   d. Olympic year should be used to promote exercise

3. Where does the author describe the changes that have occurred in the modern Olympics?

   a. paragraph 2
   b. paragraph 3
   c. paragraph 4
   d. paragraph 6

4. From the article, you can infer that the author _____ .

   a. supports raising the competitive age for females from 15 to 16
   b. believes in lowering the competitive age for females to 15
   c. doesn't feel that the age of the athletes should be considered
   d. disagrees with raising the competitive age for females from 15 to 16

5. The word *who* in the last sentence of paragraph 2 refers to _____ .

   a. philosophers
   b. moralists
   c. physicians
   d. all of the above

6. The word *if* in the last sentence of paragraph 5 signals _____ .
   a. a cause
   b. a condition
   c. a contrast
   d. a comparison

7. The word *tawdry* in paragraph 6 is closest in meaning to _____ .
   a. sophisticated
   b. cheap
   c. exciting
   d. impressive

8. The author mentions specific injuries related to each of the following sports except _____ .
   a. running
   b. gymnastics
   c. hurdling
   d. swimming

BUILDING READING SKILLS

UNDERSTANDING POINT OF VIEW

Put a check mark next to the statements you think the author would agree with.

_____ 1. The Olympic Games give sensible exercise a bad name.

_____ 2. Athletes should use drugs to enhance their performance.

_____ 3. Olympic athletes make excellent role models for the general public.

_____ 4. Olympic athletes who do not win medals are often forgotten.

_____ 5. Many Olympians will suffer long-term physical consequences from their injuries.

_____ 6. It is difficult for an Olympic athlete to have a normal family life.

_____ 7. Athletes should continue to compete even if they are in great pain.

RESPOND IN WRITING

1. You are going to write a short essay on the pros and cons of the Olympic Games. It is often easier to write about something if you talk about the subject first. In small groups, discuss the pros and cons of the Olympic Games.

2. Draw on your own experience and the information in the article to make a list of the pros and another list of the cons.

Pros	Cons

3. Use your lists of pros and cons as a guide to write a short essay describing your views on the Olympic Games.

_____

_____

_____

_____

_____

_____

_____

_____

_____

_____

_____

_____

_____

_____

_____

_____

_____

_____

_____

_____

_____

_____

_____

_____

_____

_____

_____

_____

EXPANDING VOCABULARY

Using a dictionary, write the part of speech for each word, the meaning as it is used in the article, any synonyms for the word, and a sentence to help you remember the meaning. For the last three items, choose words from the article that were unfamiliar to you.

1. blatant (¶1)

   part of speech: _____

   definition: _____

   synonyms: _____

   sentence: _____

   _____

2. reminisce (¶1)

   part of speech: _____

   definition: _____

   synonyms: _____

   sentence: _____

   _____

3. usurp (¶1)

   part of speech: _____

   definition: _____

   synonyms: _____

   sentence: _____

   _____

4. rigorous (¶2)

   part of speech: _____

   definition: _____

   synonyms: _____

   sentence: _____

   _____

5. fortify (¶2)

part of speech: _____

definition: _____

synonyms: _____

sentence: _____

_____

6. condemn (¶2)

part of speech: _____

definition: _____

synonyms: _____

sentence: _____

_____

7. pinnacle (¶4)

part of speech: _____

definition: _____

synonyms: _____

sentence: _____

_____

8. collapse (¶4)

part of speech: _____

definition: _____

synonyms: _____

sentence: _____

_____

9. discard (¶5)

part of speech: _____

definition: _____

synonyms: _____

sentence: _____

_____

10. _____ (¶   )

part of speech: _____

definition: _____

synonyms: _____

sentence: _____

_____

11. _____ (¶   )

part of speech: _____

definition: _____

synonyms: _____

sentence: _____

_____

12. _____ (¶   )

part of speech: _____

definition: _____

synonyms: _____

sentence: _____

_____

Who are today's sports heroes? From Argentina to Canada, from basketball to race car driving, "Superlatives" gives a sampling of some of the biggest names and their places in history.

SUPERLATIVES

"The greatest" is how Muhammad Ali described himself. He was right, not just because he could "float like a butterfly, sting like a bee," twice winning the heavyweight championship of the world, but because he transcended the often-sordid sport of boxing. Other sporting heroes are defined by their competitive statistics. Mr. Ali, now suffering from Parkinson's disease, is remembered for his personality.

Is America's Jack Nicklaus the world's greatest golfer? Though less magnetic than Arnold Palmer, he has won more major championships than any other golfer, including all four majors. Also the most frequent runner-up in the majors, he won his last Masters in 1986 at the age of 46. Remarkably, he was in contention to win this year's Masters as well.

Rod Laver, an unassuming Australian, is surely the best-ever tennis player: the only man to have twice won the grand slam of the game's four major tournaments—the first as an amateur in 1962, the second as a professional in 1969, a year after the open era began. However, if Pete Sampras manages a grand slam, he could displace Mr. Laver. After all, tennis in the 1990s is much more competitive than in the 1960s. Among women players, the choice is difficult. In Mr. Laver's era his equivalent was his compatriot, Margaret Court. In the modern era the Czech-born Martina Navratilova and then Germany's Steffi Graf vie for the position. But some would say the greatest of all time was America's Maureen Connolly. At the age of 18 "Little Mo" was the first woman to win a grand slam. In a four-year career cut short by injury, she entered nine majors—and won them all.

Another Australian, Don Bradman, would be a statistician's choice as the best cricketer: each time he batted for his country he seemed likely to score a century (his career average was 99.94; the next highest is 60.97). But non-statisticians would choose the West Indies' captain, Sir Garfield Sobers: not only is he the fourth-highest scorer of test centuries, but he also bowled fast-medium and spin and was a brilliant fielder.

In America's sports, Joe Montana is arguably the best football player, thanks to his play-making excellence in 15 years as a quarterback—and his knack of winning the Super Bowl for the San Francisco 49ers. Michael Jordan stands out in basketball: the highest-scoring average, an all-around game and a personality that has made the NBA a leading attraction. Babe Ruth for baseball? There are rival claimants, but Mr. Ruth took the sport to a higher level—and was brilliant as a batter, pitcher and outfielder.

In ice hockey the choice is surely Canada's Wayne Gretzky, still playing and with by far the most goals and assists. In motor racing, a sport for the brave or foolish, Juan Manuel Fangio of Argentina stands out as the only man to win five world championships. Moreover he raced in the 1950s, managing to survive an era in which car racing was much more dangerous than today.

Carl Lewis is perhaps the best track-and-field athlete of all time, not only for his nine Olympic gold medals (others have won more) but for gaining them over four successive games, from 1984 in Los Angeles to 1996 in Atlanta

And the best player of the "beautiful game"? Without a doubt Pelé himself. Not only did he score 12 goals for Brazil in four World Cups, his team winning three of them, but he pioneered soccer in America, its last frontier. Just as with Muhammad Ali, everyone, everywhere knows his name.[1]

FYI

During the Great Depression of the 1930s, baseball's Babe Ruth earned a salary of $75,000 per year—more than President Hoover's salary. When asked by reporters why he should make more money than the president, Ruth answered, "Why not? I had a better year than he did."[2]

**BUILDING
READING SKILLS**

SCANNING

Scan the article above and match the athletes with their accomplishments.

Athletes	Accomplishments
_____ 1. Joe Montana	a. won nine Olympic gold medals for track-and-field
_____ 2. Pelé	b. captain of West Indies cricket team
_____ 3. Juan Manuel Fangio	c. has won more major championships than any other golfer
_____ 4. Wayne Gretzky	d. champion Australian tennis player
_____ 5. Jack Nicklaus	e. football quarterback and Super Bowl hero
_____ 6. Carl Lewis	f. Canadian ice-hockey player with most goals and assists
_____ 7. Don Bradman	g. Brazilian soccer superstar
_____ 8. Maureen Connolly	h. Argentine race-car driver who won five world championships
_____ 9. Rod Laver	i. best Australian cricket player
_____ 10. Sir Garfield Sobers	j. first woman to win a grand slam in tennis

**BUILDING
READING SKILLS**

INCREASING
READING SPEED

You will have 20 seconds in which to underline the word that is the same as the first word in each line.

1. lick	pick	click	kick	lick	sick
2. short	sheet	tort	short	shout	shot
3. life	live	lift	life	link	file
4. jog	jug	fog	joke	dog	jog
5. last	laugh	last	fast	list	lack
6. desert	dessert	despot	despite	dispose	desert
7. fun	fury	fuse	funny	fun	fuss
8. sea	see	seem	sea	seam	seen
9. cost	stock	coast	coat	cone	cost
10. bet	bed	tab	ten	bet	best
11. save	saved	saver	sane	vase	save
12. sudden	Sunday	sullen	summer	suffer	sudden
13. task	take	task	talk	tasks	tale
14. woke	wake	woken	wolf	wok	woke
15. ticket	tickle	tickled	token	ticket	thicket

When you have finished, figure out how many answers you got right and check the appropriate box on page 263 in order to keep track of your progress.

127

POSTREADING

DISCUSSION

Read and discuss the following questions about sports.

1. "Serious sport has nothing to do with fair play. It is bound up with hatred, jealousy, boastfulness, and disregard of rules."[3] Do you agree or disagree? (George Orwell, *Shooting an Elephant*)

2. "Sports do not build character, they reveal it."[4] What does this quote mean? Do you agree? Why or why not? (Haywood Hale Broun, quoted in James Michener's *Sports in America*.)

3. Athletes have long been expected to exhibit exemplary citizenship. Why do you think this is the case? Is it fair that the public demands this of them?

4. There are no longer many differences between the worlds of sports and business. In what ways is this true? Make a list of the ways that the two "worlds" are similar and different.

5. Do athletes deserve to make more money than firefighters, doctors, or teachers? Are they worth it? In what ways?

6. Athletes are entertainers. Do others in the entertainment industry (actors and comedians, for example) deserve huge salaries? Why or why not?

JUST FOR FUN

WORD PLAY

The question WHAT'S A ROLE MODEL? contains fifteen letters. Using only these letters, make as many words of two or more letters as you can. You may not use the same letter twice unless it appears twice in the question. Do not use proper names or foreign words.

_____   _____   _____

_____   _____   _____

_____   _____   _____

_____   _____   _____

_____   _____   _____

_____   _____   _____

_____   _____   _____

_____   _____   _____

_____   _____   _____

_____   _____   _____

_____   _____   _____

_____   _____   _____

_____   _____   _____

_____   _____   _____

READER'S JOURNAL

Choose a topic that relates to the readings in this unit and write for about ten to twenty minutes. Consider using one of the quotes or one of the discussion questions in this unit as the basis for your writing.

READER'S JOURNAL

Date: _____

_____

_____

_____

_____

_____

_____

_____

_____

_____

_____

_____

_____

_____

_____

_____

_____

_____

_____

_____

_____

_____

_____

YOUR PLACE IN THE FAMILY

FYi

Unit·5

Selections

Scientists and social scientists have long been interested in the investigation of what factors determine personality traits. Among the factors that have been studied are genes, environment, age, and gender. Now a new theory asserts that position in the family (birth order) is the most reliable indicator of personality. In this unit you will read about this fascinating theory and its application to the world of business.

POINTS TO
PONDER

Think about and then discuss the following questions.

1. What factors do you think affect a person's personality?

2. Do you have any siblings? In what ways are you similar to or different from them?

3. When you think of the word *family,* what comes to mind? Freewrite for ten minutes on the topic of family. Write as much as you can as fast as you can without worrying about mistakes.

_____

_____

_____

_____

_____

_____

_____

_____

_____

_____

_____

_____

_____

_____

Frank Sulloway is a researcher at the Massachusetts Institute of Technology. After spending over twenty-five years analyzing more than 6,000 people (mostly historical figures involved in scientific breakthroughs and historic revolutions), he found that birth order is more important in shaping personality than gender, race, nationality or social class. He even believes that those occupying the same birth rank have more in common with each other than they do with their own siblings. In the following interview, "Rebels Among Us: Birth Order and Personality," Sulloway answers some thought-provoking questions about the effects of birth order. As you read the interview, think about your own birth order and your relationships with siblings and friends.

BEFORE YOU READ

PREREADING ACTIVITY

Form three groups according to birth order as follows:

    Group 1: All those who are firstborns and only children

    Group 2: All those who are middle children

    Group 3: All those who are laterborns

Work together to make a list of five personality traits that members of your group have in common. Choose one member from each group to write the list on the board. Discuss the similarities and differences among the three lists.

● ●

Rebels Among Us: Birth Order and Personality

BY KAREN LINDELL

1   *Y*our kids might share the same curly hair and Mom's blue eyes, but why are they so different when it comes to personality? According to a new theory by Frank Sulloway, a research scholar at the Massachusetts Institute of Technology and author of *Born to Rebel: Birth Order, Family Dynamics, and Creative Lives* (Pantheon Books), what creates such

dissimilarity among siblings is their place in the family structure. Sulloway spent 20 years gathering biographical data on more than 6,000 people involved in scientific and historic revolutions, and he reviewed 196 studies on the effects of birth order. He found that firstborns were significantly more likely to be conservative reactionaries who defended the status quo, while laterborns were more likely to be radical rebels who questioned or overthrew it.

2   You're probably not raising the next Charles Darwin or Joan of Arc (both laterborns), but Sulloway's theory applies to less eminent folk as well. He claims that by differentiating themselves from each other, siblings are more likely to gain attention from parents, which in turn increases their chances of surviving childhood. So sibling rivalry isn't just your kids' attempt to annoy you—it's a survival tactic to grab your attention. In an interview with *L.A. Parent*, Sulloway discusses why—according to his theory—your eldest was born to boss and your youngest may turn out be a rebel with a cause.

3   **Q:** What can parents expect from a firstborn? A laterborn?
A: Firstborns and laterborns differ in predictable ways because they occupy different "niches" within the family. Firstborns have a special niche as the eldest in the family. As such, they tend to identify more with parents. They act as surrogate parents to younger siblings, and they're more assertive, dominant, conscientious, conventional, serious and adult-like. They're the "goody-goody" of the family. Annette Funicello and Jimmy Carter, for example, were firstborns.

4   Laterborns look for new and different ways to impress parents because the parent-identified niche is taken. Laterborns are less conforming, more open to new experiences and more likely to take risks. Because they can't use the advantage of greater physical size (like their older siblings), laterborns are more sociable, flexible, and democratic. Laterborns also use a sense of humor as a way of getting attention. It's interesting that laterborns are more likely to become comedians, while firstborns are more likely to become dramatic actors. Sylvester Stallone, John Wayne, and Clint Eastwood are firstborns; Charlie Chaplin, Bob Hope, and Jay Leno are laterborns.

5   **Q:** Are children destined to form a particular birth-order personality, even if their parents deliberately try not to show favoritism?
A: Kids want to make sure they're being treated equally. Even if parents somehow miraculously treat each child the same, siblings are constantly testing the waters to see if things have changed, and they'll try to provoke the system. If parents do discriminate, it breeds even greater rivalry.

6   It's important for parents to know that sibling rivalry is not their fault—it's been around for millions of years, and it's the normal Darwinian process by which children survive childhood. Particularly for young children, sibling competition is also a very creative process. It's part of the process by which they become themselves—unique individuals.

7   **Q:** Do even very young children exhibit this competition for parental favor?
A: In a biological sense, sibling competition begins at birth, when newborns are breastfeeding. Breastfeeding is an effective contraceptive device because

it puts off the date of having another sibling to compete for parental attention. At a psychological level, we know from studies of very young children that at an early age—as early as eight months—children are acutely aware of parents showing attention toward another sibling. After the first year of birth, birth order begins to shape the strategies siblings use to gain parental favor. Studies have shown that the influence of birth order is manifest by ages five and six.

8 **Q:** If siblings are always competing with each other, how do you account for siblings who are close, regardless of whether their personalities are similar or different?
A: Siblings will generally, but not always, compete with each other. They will also cooperate when that's a good strategy. After all, siblings do share half their genes and will sometimes even give their lives for each other. And identical twins, who share all their genes, are especially entwined in each other's lives. If parents don't have any resources to give, then it makes more sense for siblings to pool resources. This is often the case for poor families. In normal families, siblings both compete and cooperate all the time.

9 **Q:** Do males and females adopt different strategies to gain parents' attention?
A: The style of sibling competition is influenced independently by gender. Males are more aggressive than females, and firstborn males are more aggressive than firstborn females. But female firstborns are more aggressive than their younger brothers. Traits that are related to gender can also be explained by birth order. We need to use both birth order and gender to understand personality.

10 **Q:** What about only children and middle children? Are they more like firstborns or laterborns, or are they a special case?
A: Only children obviously have no siblings and don't experience any rivalry. Because they're free to occupy any niche they want, they can experiment. They're the most unpredictable of all sibling groups because they're not limited by birth order.

11 Middle children are more like laterborns when it comes to traits such as openness to experience, but because of the unique niche they occupy, middleborns are the least likely of any sibling type to use aggression. Unlike firstborns, they're not the biggest, and unlike the youngest sibling, they may not be protected by parents as the "baby" of the family. Because middleborns don't have these advantages, they're more cooperative, diplomatic, and willing to compromise.

12 **Q:** How do you account for exceptions to your theory?
A: Birth order doesn't explain everything. Gender, temperament and how well siblings get along with their parents are also important variables. For example, firstborn males are more physically aggressive than firstborn females, and shy laterborns are less radical than extroverted laterborns. And firstborns who experience conflict with parents are more likely be rebellious than conforming. The largest source of exception is genetic differences—genes account for 30 to 40 percent of most variances in personality traits. So shyness, which is a heritable trait, may mask some birth-order

effects. Birth order can correctly account for what 70 percent of the population will do, and additional environmental or genetic influences account for another 15 percent. As for the other 15 percent, no theory can consider every possible environmental factor. Even with all the variance, it's amazing that we can predict what 85 percent of the population will be like.

The Ranks of the Famous

Firstborns	Laterborns
Bill (and Hillary) Clinton	Martin Luther King Jr.
Oprah Winfrey	Fidel Castro
Winston Churchill	Madonna
Rush Limbaugh	Benjamin Franklin
Joseph Stalin	Harriet Tubman
Peter Jennings	Bill Gates
	Gloria Steinem

● ●

HOW WELL DID YOU READ?

According to Frank Sulloway, which traits are more characteristic of first-borns? Which ones are more characteristic of laterborns? Complete the chart.

democratic
dominant
open to new experiences
conscientious
defends the status quo
sociable
takes risks

conventional
flexible
assertive
rebels against the status quo
adult-like
serious
less conforming

Firstborn	Laterborn
assertive serious.	sociable
dominant	flexible
conscientious	democratic
conventional / conservative	rebels against status quo
bossy	open to new experiences.
mature acting	takes turn
defends status quo.	less conservative

adult-like.

"right wing"   *"left wing"*

BUILDING READING SKILLS

UNDERSTANDING POINT OF VIEW

Put a check mark next to the statements you think Frank Sulloway would agree with.

_____ 1. It is easy to predict the differences in personality between firstborns and laterborns.

_____ 2. It is impossible for a single theory to take every environmental factor into account.

_____ 3. Only children are not as predictable as firstborns.

_____ 4. It is easy for parents to treat each child in the same way.

_____ 5. Among siblings, competition is always a more effective strategy than cooperation.

_____ 6. Although personality is affected by several factors, birth order is the most significant determinant.

_____ 7. A firstborn child would be more likely to become an accountant than a laterborn child.

_____ 8. Middle children are more likely to get into fights at school than laterborn children.

_____ 9. Parents are responsible for sibling rivalry among their children.

EXPANDING VOCABULARY

Using a dictionary, write the part of speech for each word, the meaning as it is used in the article, any synonyms for the word, and a sentence to help you remember the meaning. For the last three items, choose words from the article that were unfamiliar to you.

1. conservative (¶1)

   part of speech: _____

   definition: _____

   synonyms: _____

   sentence: _____

   _____

2. eminent (¶2)

   part of speech: _____

   definition: _____

   synonyms: _____

   sentence: _____

   _____

3. surrogate (¶3)

   part of speech: _____

   definition: _____

   synonyms: _____

   sentence: _____

   _____

4. miraculously (¶5)

   part of speech: _____

   definition: _____

   synonyms: _____

   sentence: _____

   _____

5. provoke (¶5)

   part of speech: _____

   definition: _____

   synonyms: _____

   sentence: _____

   _____

6. discriminate (¶5)

   part of speech: _____

   definition: _____

   synonyms: _____

   sentence: _____

   _____

7. diplomatic (¶11)

   part of speech: _____

   definition: _____

   synonyms: _____

   sentence: _____

   _____

8. _____ (¶   )

part of speech: _____

definition: _____

synonyms: _____

sentence: _____

_____

9. _____ (¶   )

part of speech: _____

definition: _____

synonyms: _____

sentence: _____

_____

10. _____ (¶   )

part of speech: _____

definition: _____

synonyms: _____

sentence: _____

_____

BUILDING WRITING SKILLS

SUMMARIZING

In the interview, Frank Sulloway discusses the differences between first-borns and laterborns. In your own words, summarize Sulloway's theory.

_____

_____

_____

_____

_____

_____

_____

_____

_____

TALK IT OVER

DISCUSSION

With the members of your original birth order group formed for the Prereading activity on page 133, review the notes from your first discussion in light of what you have learned about Sulloway's theory of birth order. Do the members of your group fit his description of firstborns or laterborns? Do most people in your group share the characteristics Sulloway attributed to firstborns or laterborns?

BUILDING READING SKILLS

INCREASING READING SPEED

You will have 20 seconds in which to underline the word that is the same as the first word in each line.

1. shape	shade	ship	shrink	shape	drape
2. man	mean	main	new	man	men
3. disk	desk	skid	disk	dust	sick
4. favor	major	flavor	fever	favor	fight
5. should	would	should	could	foul	shook
6. dot	pot	does	dot	ton	do
7. might	may	must	mint	maybe	might
8. key	key	keel	kill	kick	keep
9. duty	duly	dusk	dust	duty	due
10. gas	fast	sag	gas	shag	gash
11. let	let's	lethal	level	let	leg
12. begun	begrudge	behave	begin	beguile	begun
13. redden	read	dear	redden	ran	red
14. little	litter	little	lithe	livid	like
15. record	recount	recoup	recreate	record	reek

When you have finished, figure out how many answers you got right and check the appropriate box on page 263 in order to keep track of your progress.

In *Born to Rebel,* Frank J. Sulloway argues that laterborn children are more innovative and adventurous than firstborns. Though his studies have focused on political and scientific revolutions, Mr. Sulloway thinks the hypothesis holds for business executives as well. In the following article, "A Telling Birthmark For Businesses," Judith H. Dobrzynski examines Sulloway's theory that too many firstborn men rule the nation's corporations. Skeptics say he makes too many generalizations to support his premise.

BEFORE YOU READ
_____
PREREADING DISCUSSION

1. What is the mental picture you have of someone who is the chief executive officer (CEO) of a company? What qualities do you think make someone a good CEO? Do you think he or she is more likely to be a firstborn or a laterborn?

2. Do you believe in Sulloway's theories, or are you skeptical of them?

● ●

A Telling Birthmark For Businesses

Researcher Says How C.E.O.'s Act Is Linked to Order in the Family

BY JUDITH H. DOBRZYNSKI

1 It is a classic management problem. A company is rolling along, unaware that the bumps it is hitting signal the need to change the way it does business. It isn't really broke, the chief executive thinks, so there's no need to fix it. A little tinkering will do the trick.

2 But as company after company— from Eastman Kodak to General Motors to I.B.M.—has shown, that way lies disaster.

3 The mystery is why so few smart, worldly wise chief executives see the need to foment a corporate revolution before disaster hits.

4 Frank J. Sulloway has a theory: Too many first-born men rule the nation's corporations. First-born children, he thinks, based on 26 years or research,

are authoritarian conformists, assiduously interested in preserving the status quo. Later-borns are more adventurous and receptive to innovation.

5   "Whenever something really drastic is required, it's always more difficult for a first-born to do it," said Mr. Sulloway, a science historian and research scholar at the Massachusetts Institute of Technology who has amassed a huge data base that he says proves his point statistically. "That means they'll be doing it later than they should."

6   "Strategy," he said, "is something that later-borns ought to be superior at compared with first-borns, who are in turn more adept at managing than at strategic overhauls."

7   Mr. Sulloway, who—no surprise—is the third of four children, ignited something of his own revolution last fall when he published *Born to Rebel: Birth Order, Family Dynamics, and Creative Lives* (Pantheon). In it, he argued that birth order was the most reliable predictor of openness to innovation and social change.

8   That conclusion was based on Mr. Sulloway's analysis of a data base he built of 6,566 people who participated in 121 political and scientific upheavals, including the French Revolution, the emergence of Darwin's theory of evolution and the Protestant Reformation.

9   To determine who is most likely, in any era, to challenge the established wisdom, he studied as many as 256 characteristics, like age, religion, class, education and travel experience.

10   "Birth order was the best predictor," he discovered.

11   While he has not systematically studied business executives, Mr. Sulloway said the message for companies was clear.

12   People who select chief executives, he contends, would do well to consider candidates' birth order, among other variables, especially if radical change is required. And he thinks corporate boards probably have too high a proportion of first-borns, too, adding to the chief executive's tendency to delay needed change.

13   To later-borns who are tired of seeing their older siblings rule so many roosts, meanwhile, Mr. Sulloway's work offers an encouraging note—if, as some management experts think, the authoritarian management model has had its day.

14   "If command-and-control management is out, it's great news for later-borns," Mr. Sulloway predicted. "They'll move up in the corporation." And that would be good, he said, because later-borns in general are more agreeable than their eldest siblings, less defensive about errors, less territorial and more sympathetic to underdogs and underlings.

15   His notion that birth order—and the ensuing dynamics among parents and children—shapes personalities, who then shape history, is a variation on previous birth-order research, which some social scientists consider dubious.

16   Mr. Sulloway offers his own cautions. His research showed that two characteristics other than birth order were nearly as important as predictors of the propensity to rebel: "Age and the social attitude of the family, and hence your own social attitude." Younger people tend to be more open to the new because they have less stake in the established, Mr. Sulloway said, and children tend to draw social attitudes from their parents.

17   Even so, one key-factor can disrupt the pattern, he said—a bad relationship between a child and his parents. Nor is his analytical framework failsafe: the behavior of 15 percent of the population defies explanation.

18   Mr. Sulloway's caveats, however, did not stop the potshots. Writing in The New Republic, Alan Wolfe, a sociology professor at Boston University, credited Mr. Sulloway for "establishing the importance of birth order," but questioned his objectivity and criticized him for relying on the assumption that family dynamics have been stable throughout history. Mr. Wolfe's scorching review branded the book "powerful rhetoric" and "bad science."

19   In any case, people are buying the 653-page tome. It is in its fourth printing, with 56,000 copies in circulation.

20   Despite the limits of his research, Mr. Sulloway thinks his work has relevance for spheres he has not studied closely, including business. "I can say a lot about people I don't know personally," he said. His analyses take off from a person's position as a first-born or later-born but go deeper into family dynamics, considering variables like sex, the number and sex of siblings and the age spacing between them.

21   At the recent World Economic Forum meeting in Davos, Switzerland, the panel Mr. Sulloway led on his work was standing room only, packed with believers and skeptics alike. Lester Thurow, the M.I.T. economist and former dean of its Sloan School of Management, was on the panel. "It's all very fascinating," Mr. Thurow said later, "and, like 'survival of the fittest,' on some level it just seems right. But there are always exceptions, so it's too conditional. You can't use it to make decisions."

22   Besides, Mr. Thurow pointed out, just because later-borns tend to rebel does not mean that they discriminate between good and bad revolutions.

23   Until the forum meeting, Mr. Sulloway's work had hardly registered in the business world. He has not heard from any corporations. "I'm quite surprised, because of the implications of the book regarding the adaptability to change," he said.

24 But that itself may change. Nan-b de Gaspé Beaubien, president of the Institute for Family Enterprise in Canada, is exploring additional research with Mr. Sulloway. John O'Neil, another forum panelist who is president of the Center for Leadership Renewal, a consulting and training firm in San Francisco, said he would help Mr. Sulloway determine whether his work could have practical use in corporations.

25 Meantime, between media interviews, Mr. Sulloway is starting on the task unsystematically, mainly in response to inquiries. At the request of The New York Times, he examined biographical material and news reports about three executives—Louis V. Gerstner, the chairman of I.B.M., Gerald M. Levin, the chairman of Time Warner Inc., and Albert J. Dunlap, the chairman of the Sunbeam Corporation.

Later-borns may have their day if a new management model emerges.

26 Fittingly, Mr. Gerstner, the second of four sons, has overseen dramatic changes at both RJR Nabisco and I.B.M. Both involved cultural revolutions, but with distinctly different characters. At RJR, he reined in a free-wheeling corporate culture and managed to pay down a stupendous debt load without selling many assets. At I.B.M., he freed a stodgy bureaucracy.

27 The contrast showed his adaptability. Mr. Sulloway said, a trait of later-borns that pops up many times in Mr. Gerstner's career. The linch-pin of Mr. Gerstner's prescription for I.B.M.—customer focus—is a distinct turn-around from I.B.M.'s recent past and equally telling. "By making an effort to learn about his customers' needs, rather than dictating to them from a position of technological superiority, he emphasized the later-borns' ability to identify with their peers," Mr. Sulloway said "Later-borns like to get out there—to find out what employees think and what customers think."

28 Mr. Levin, the third of three children, also fits the mold. "Typical of later-borns, he is soft-spoken—an ordinary guy with a relative absence of charisma." Mr. Sulloway said. "He combines an easygoing personal style with surprising tenacity and a marked penchant for risk-taking." Some recent evidence: Time Warner's purchase of the Turner Broadcasting Company, even while Mr. Levin struggles to get Time Warner's existing fiefs to act as one company.

29 Also predictable for a later-born, Mr. Sulloway said, is Mr. Levin's record as a contrarian, a man of ideas and strategy. Those traits came to light in the mid-1970's, when he put Home Box Office on satellite, a breakthrough at the time. More recently, it is reflected in his commitment to cable television, no matter the potential for near-term losses and pressures to sell cable properties to pay down the company's gargantuan debt.

30 Mr. Dunlap is a more complicated case. Renowned for his ambition, aggression and arrogance, Mr. Dunlap in many ways epitomizes a first-born, which he is. In masterminding his corporate restructurings, most recently at Scott Paper and Sunbeam, he has decimated the work force. Proud of being tough-minded—he called his book "Mean Business"—he makes huge demands on minions.

31 But he is also an iconoclast, caring little about the established order, which seems out of step with his family position.

[32] Mr. Sulloway is quick to explain. "In many ways, Mr. Dunlap's brash temperament—which is extreme even for a first-born—makes him something of a nonconformist, one who cares little for corporate authority precisely because he is so taken with himself," Mr. Sulloway said. "If Dunlap is a rebel, it is out of arrogance rather than empathy for the underdog, and hence a result of love of domination rather than a liberating resentment against it." He chalks up Mr. Dunlap's behavior to his troubled relationship with his family, which has been widely chronicled.

[33] Despite its ring of generalization or pop psychology, detailed birth-order analyses could help boards choose chief executives, once they have blocked out the characteristics needed to do the job, Mr. Sulloway suggests. And board nominating committees, too, might do well to include people who vary by birth order, not just indus-

try background and expertise, he said.

[34] The idea is not so crazy. "When I interview candidates, I ask questions that get at their early background, including the number of their brothers and sisters," said Michael A. Wellman, managing director of the New York office of Korn/Ferry international, an executive recruitment firm. "It's another part of the subjective information we use to get a handle on them." However, he said, it, like body language, was less important than things like industry knowledge, experience, management style and reputation.

[35] Mr. O'Neil, the leadership consultant, has a less grand view of how Mr. Sulloway's research may help.

[36] "Family is a place where a lot of people get stuck," he said. "We get stuck with family stories, and they get embedded in our behavior. Sometimes that can hurt us. This may help us think through how we view our roles and how we write our next chapters."

● ●

HOW WELL DID YOU READ?

A. Circle the letter of the choice that best completes the sentence or answers the question.

1. The main purpose of this article is to _____ .

   a. persuade readers to hire laterborn chief executives
   b. entertain readers with stories about mistakes that some chief executive officers have made
   c. inform readers about a theory that links chief executives' behavior with birth order
   d. make predictions about the success of Sulloway's theory

2. What word best describes the author's tone?

   a. objective
   b. insulting
   c. sentimental
   d. disbelieving

3. Mr. Sulloway cites *age* and *social attitude* as _____ .

    a. irrelevant factors in determining personality
    b. other predictors of personality
    c. the most important factors in family dynamics
    d. examples of personality traits

4. Where in the article does the author mention a negative review of Sulloway's book?

    a. paragraph 18
    b. paragraph 19
    c. paragraph 20
    d. paragraph 28

5. According to Sulloway, 15 percent of the population _____ .

    a. have bad relationships with their parents
    b. agree with his theory
    c. have the propensity to rebel
    d. do not fit his model

6. According to Sulloway, which of the following is not generally a characteristic of laterborns?

    a. They are less defensive about errors.
    b. They are more agreeable than their eldest siblings.
    c. They are more ambitious than their siblings.
    d. They are less territorial and more sympathetic to underlings.

B. Read the following statements. If a statement is true, write *T* on the line. If it is false, write *F*.

_____ 1. Frank Sulloway has systematically studied the personality traits of business executives.

_____ 2. Some social scientists have reservations about the theory that birth order shapes personality.

_____ 3. Alan Wolfe's review of *Born to Rebel* was critical.

_____ 4. According to Sulloway, companies that need a strategic overhaul should consider hiring executives who are firstborns.

_____ 5. Frank Sulloway is the first person to research the effects of birth order on personality.

_____ 6. Mr. Sulloway's research has had a great impact on the business world.

**RESPOND IN
WRITING**

In your own words, explain how Sulloway's theory of birth order can be
related to the performance of business executives. Then explain whether
you think it is appropriate to apply Sulloway's theory to business executives. Give specific reasons to support your position.

_____

_____

_____

_____

_____

_____

_____

_____

_____

_____

_____

**BUILDING
READING SKILLS**

UNDERSTANDING
TRANSITIONS

Words and phrases that show the relationship between ideas, sentences, and
paragraphs are called _transitions_. Study the chart below.

Transitions

Time: Used to show the order in which events happen

first	originally	later	now that
second	at the same time as	subsequently	since
third	just as	as soon as	once
next	while	when	until
finally	during	before	by the time that
at present		after	whenever
now			

Addition: Used to add another idea

also	besides	furthermore	moreover
and	finally	in addition	next
another	first	in addition to	second

Cause and effect: Used to express the cause or effect (result) of something

as	because of	inasmuch as	so
as a result	consequently	now that	therefore
as a result of	due to	on account of	thus
because	hence	since	

Comparison: Used to show similarities between and among things

as	in a similar fashion	just as	likewise
as well	in the same way	like	similarly
equally			

Contrast: Used to show differences between and among things

but	instead of	still	while
however	on the other hand	whereas	yet
in contrast	rather than		

Condition: Used to tell what must happen in order for something else to take place

as long as	otherwise	suppose	unless
if	provided that		

Concession: Used to describe an unexpected result

although	even though	nevertheless	still
despite	however	nonetheless	though
even if	in spite of		

Illustration: Used to give examples

for example	including	like	such as
for instance			

Purpose: Used to show intent

for	in order that	so that

Read the following sentences and underline the transitions. Write the transition word(s) on the line, and identify the type of relationship signified.

1. *To determine who is most likely, in any era, to challenge the established wisdom, he studied as many as 256 characteristics, like age, religion, class, education and travel experience.*

   Transition: _____ like _____

   Type of relationship: _____ comparison _____

2. *While he has not systematically studied business executives, Mr. Sulloway said the message for companies was clear.*

   Transition: _____ while _____

   Type of relationship: _____ contrast _____

3. *People who select chief executives, he contends, would do well to consider candidates' birth order, among other variables, especially if radical change is required.*

   Transition: _____ if _____

   Type of relationship: _____ condition _____

4. *Younger people tend to be more open to the new because they have less stake in the established . . .*

   Transition: _____ because _____

   Type of relationship: _____ cause & effect _____

5. *Mr. Sulloway's caveats, however, did not stop the potshots.*

   Transition: _____ however _____

   Type of relationship: _____ contrast _____

6. *Despite the limits of his research, Mr. Sulloway thinks his work has relevance to spheres he has not studied closely, including business.*

   Transition: _____ despite _____

   Type of relationship: _____ concession _____

7. *Besides, Mr. Thurow pointed out, just because later-borns tend to rebel does not mean they discriminate between good and bad revolutions.*

   Transition: _____ besides _____

   Type of relationship: _____ addition _____

8. *Until the forum meeting, Mr. Sulloway's work had hardly registered in the business world.*

   Transition: _____ until _____

   Type of relationship: _____ time _____

BUILDING READING SKILLS

UNDERSTANDING REFERENCES

Write the word or phrase that the highlighted reference refers to.

1. *His notion that birth order—and the ensuing dynamics among parents and children—shapes personalities, **who** then shape history, is a variation on previous birth-order research, **which** some social scientists consider dubious.*

   who = _personalities_

   which = _birth order research_

2. *In Born to Rebel: Birth Order, Family Dynamics, and Creative Lives, Sulloway argued that birth order was the most reliable predictor of openness to innovation and social change. **That conclusion** was based on Mr. Sulloway's analysis of a data base he built of 6,566 people who participated in 121 political and scientific upheavals . . .*

   That conclusion = _birth order ... social change_

3. *"If command-and-control management is out, it's great news for later-borns," Mr. Sulloway predicted. "**They**'ll move up in the corporation."*

   They = _later-borns_

4. *Fittingly, Mr. Gerstner, the second of four sons, has overseen dramatic changes at both RJR Nabisco and I.B.M. **Both** involved cultural revolutions, but with distinctly different characters.*

   Both = _RJR Nabisco & IBM_

5. *"Whenever something really drastic is required, it's always more difficult for a first-born to do **it**," said Mr. Sulloway, a science historian and research scholar at the Massachusetts Institute of Technology who has amassed a huge data base that he says proves **his point** statistically.*

   it = _something really drastic_

   his point = _whenever something drastic ...... to do it_

6. *Also predictable for a later-born, Mr. Sulloway said, is Mr. Levin's record as a contrarian, a man of ideas and strategy. **Those traits** came to light in the mid-1970s, when he put Home Box Office on satellite, a breakthrough at the time.*

   Those traits = _Contrarian, man of ideas and strategy_

**EXPANDING
VOCABULARY**

Using a dictionary, write the part of speech for each word, the meaning as it is used in the article, any synonyms for the word, and a sentence to help you remember the meaning. For the last two items, choose words from the article that were unfamiliar to you.

1. predictor (¶10)

   part of speech: _____

   definition: _____

   synonyms: _____

   sentence: _____

   _____

2. contend (¶12)

   part of speech: _____

   definition: _____

   synonyms: _____

   sentence: _____

   _____

3. dubious (¶15)

   part of speech: _____

   definition: _____

   synonyms: _____

   sentence: _____

   _____

4. sympathetic (¶14)

   part of speech: _____

   definition: _____

   synonyms: _____

   sentence: _____

   _____

5. disrupt (¶17)

    part of speech: _____

    definition: _____

    synonyms: _____

    sentence: _____

    _____

6. analytical (¶17)

    part of speech: _____

    definition: _____

    synonyms: _____

    sentence: _____

    _____

7. assumption (¶18)

    part of speech: _____

    definition: _____

    synonyms: _____

    sentence: _____

    _____

8. skeptic (¶21)

    part of speech: _____

    definition: _____

    synonyms: _____

    sentence: _____

    _____

9. discriminate (¶22)

    part of speech: _____

    definition: _____

    synonyms: _____

    sentence: _____

    _____

10. adaptability (¶27)

   part of speech: _____

   definition: _____

   synonyms: _____

   sentence: _____

   _____

11. iconoclast (¶31)

   part of speech: _____

   definition: _____

   synonyms: _____

   sentence: _____

   _____

12. _____ (¶   )

   part of speech: _____

   definition: _____

   synonyms: _____

   sentence: _____

   _____

13. _____ (¶   )

   part of speech: _____

   definition: _____

   synonyms: _____

   sentence: _____

   _____

Richard Shelton is the author of nine books of poetry. He has also written scripts for several short documentary films, nonfiction books, and short stories, such as "The Stones." His poems and prose pieces have been published in more than 200 magazines and journals; translated into Spanish, French, Swedish, Polish, and Japanese; and set to music by composers. Since 1972, Shelton has taught writers' workshops in the Arizona prisons. Eight books of poetry and prose by men in these workshops have been published.

BEFORE YOU READ

PREREADING DISCUSSION

1. Do you prefer to read fiction or nonfiction?

2. Do you prefer to read novels, short stories, or poems?

3. Read the first paragraph of the story. What do you think the stones represent?

● ●

The Stones

BY RICHARD SHELTON

1   I love to go out on summer nights and watch the stones grow. I think they grow better here in the desert, where it is warm and dry, than almost anywhere else. Or perhaps it is only that the young ones are more active here.

2   Young stones tend to move about more than their elders consider good for them. Most young stones have a secret desire which their parents had before them but have forgotten ages ago. And because this desire involves water, it is never mentioned. The older stones disapprove of water and say, "Water is a gadfly who never stays in one place long enough to learn anything." But the young stones try to work themselves into a position, slowly and without their elders noticing it, in which a sizable stream of water during a summer storm might catch them broadside and unknowing, so to speak, and push them along over a slope or down an arroyo. In spite of the danger this involves, they want to travel and see something of the world and settle in a new place, far from home, where they can raise their own dynasties away from the domination of their parents.

3   And although family ties are very strong among stones, many of the more daring young ones have succeeded, and they carry scars to prove to their children that they once went on a journey, helter-skelter and high water, and traveled perhaps fifteen feet, an incredible distance. As they grow older, they cease to brag about such clandestine adventures.

4   It is true that old stones get to be very conservative. They consider all movement either dangerous or downright sinful. They remain comfortable where they are and often get fat. Fatness, as a matter of fact, is a mark of distinction.

5   And on summer nights, after the young stones are asleep, the elders turn to a serious and frightening subject—the moon, which is always spoken of in whispers. "See how it glows and whips across the sky, always changing its shape," one says. And another says, "Feel how it pulls at us, urging us to follow." And a third whispers, "It is a stone gone mad."

HOW WELL DID YOU READ?

1. How does the author describe old stones?

¶ 4 conservative – consider movement sinful

comfy   fat

2. How does the author describe young stones?

Move more than elders think good

have secret desires

3. Where does the story take place?

   in the desert

4. What secret desire do the young stones have?

   travel - see the world
   settle in a new place

5. Why do the young stones want to settle in a new place?

   raise own 'dynasties' away from
   parental 'domination'

6. What do the old stones think about water?

   disapprove

7. In what ways do the stones change as they get older?

   forget desire to travel - cease to brag about
   youth

8. What is a mark of distinction for the old stones?

   Scars from journeys

9. Why do the old stones believe that the moon is a stone gone mad?

   glows - whisps across sky, always
   changing shape & pulling other stones after it.

**BUILDING
READING SKILLS**

UNDERSTANDING
FIGURATIVE
LANGUAGE

Authors often use *figurative language* such as *similes*, *metaphors*, and *personification* to make their writing more vivid. Study the chart below.

Simile   An expression in which two things are compared by using the words *like* or *as*.

Example: He was so scared that his face turned white as snow.

Metaphor   A way of describing something by comparing it to something else that has similar qualities, without using the words *like* or *as*.

Example: I cried a river of tears.

Personification   Representation of inanimate objects or abstract ideas as living beings.

Example: Justice is blind.

Which of these literary techniques has Richard Sheldon used in "The Stones"?

_____

Read the following sentences that use figurative language. Write an *S* if the sentence is an example of a simile, write an *M* if it is a metaphor, and write a *P* if it shows personification.

_____   1. The rain came down in buckets.

_____   2. My thoughts are as deep as the deepest ocean.

_____   3. Happiness is a flower that blossoms in my heart.

_____   4. "All the world's a stage, and all the men and women merely players." (William Shakespeare)

_____   5. "Hope is a thing with feathers." (Emily Dickinson)

_____   6. "She's a wild horse of a woman." (Sandra Cisneros)

_____   7. The stars danced lightly across the sky.

_____   8. "My love is like a red, red rose." (Robert Burns)

_____   9. "It's small and red with tight steps in front and windows so small you'd think they were holding their breath." (Sandra Cisneros)

_____   10. She flew like a bird.

_____   11. "Time is the thief of youth." (John Milton)

_____   12. The bad news was like a knife in her heart.

_____   13. His words were music to my ears.

_____   14. The moon looked down and smiled at me.

_____   15. The angry ocean battled with the houses on the shore.

157

1. Did you like this story? Why or why not?

2. If you had written this story, what would you have used as a title?

3. What is the meaning behind this story? In other words, what do you think was Richard Sheldon's purpose in writing it?

4. Did you find the story to be optimistic? pessimistic? prophetic? humorous? cautionary?

5. What is your emotional reaction to the story? How did it make you feel?

6. What do you think of when you look at the moon?

RESPOND IN WRITING

In the story, you read that "Most young stones have a secret desire which their parents had before them but have forgotten ages ago." Write a paragraph about your secret desire.

_____

_____

_____

_____

_____

_____

_____

_____

_____

_____

_____

_____

_____

_____

_____

_____

_____

_____

POSTREADING

DISCUSSION

1. "If we are the younger, we may envy the older. If we are the older, we may feel that the younger is always being indulged. In other words, no matter what position we hold in family birth order, we can prove beyond a doubt that we are being gypped."[1] Is this true for you? (Judith Viorst, *Necessary Losses*)

2. "In families, children tend to take on stock roles, as if there were hats hung up in some secret place, visible only to the children. Each succeeding child selects a hat and takes on that role: the good child, the black sheep, the clown, and so on."[2] Now that you have completed the readings in this unit, what is your reaction to this quote? (Ellen Galinsky, *Between Generations*)

3. "Being in a family is like being in a play. Each birth order position is like a different part in a play, with distinct and separate characters for each part. Therefore, if one sibling has already filled a part, such as the good child, other siblings may feel they have to find other parts to play, such as the rebellious child, academic child, athletic child, social child and so on."[3] Do you agree with this assessment of family life? What is your role in your own family? (Jane Nelson, *Positive Discipline*)

JUST FOR FUN

ANAGRAM

Make as many words as you can by using the letters in the boxes. However, the letter "a" must occur in every word you make. Proper nouns and non-English words are not allowed. Write your words in the spaces below. Compare your list with your classmates' lists.

1. _____
2. _____
3. _____
4. _____
5. _____
6. _____
7. _____
8. _____
9. _____
10. _____

A	L	B	
T	I	L	A
O	I	Z	
O	G	N	

READER'S JOURNAL

Choose a topic that relates to the readings in this unit, and write for about ten to twenty minutes. Consider using one of the quotes or one of the discussion questions in this unit as the basis for your writing.

READER'S JOURNAL

Date: _____

INFLUENTIAL ENTERTAINERS

Selections

Television is a powerful medium that has the ability to influence our lives and affect society. There are many famous TV personalities, but only a handful of them have truly changed their medium. This unit contains articles about three such influential TV personalities: Oprah Winfrey, Lucille Ball, and Jim Henson.

DISCUSSION

Think about and then discuss the following questions.

1. What type of TV shows do you enjoy the most? Rank the following types 1–5. 1 = your favorite type, and 5 = your least favorite.

   _____ situation comedy

   _____ soap opera

   _____ news

   _____ sports

   _____ talk show

2. How much TV do you watch per week?

3. What is your definition of the word *entertainment*?

4. Would you like to be a celebrity? Why or why not?

Oprah Winfrey is much more than just the exceedingly popular host of a television talk show. She is also a producer, author, actress, businesswoman, and philanthropist. And she is not just good, but very good, at everything she does. In the following article, "The TV Host: Oprah Winfrey," Deborah Tannen discusses the profound influence Oprah Winfrey has on audiences all over the world.

Tannen is a well-known professor, researcher, and author in the field of sociolinguistics. Her books include *You Just Don't Understand: Men and Women in Conversation* (1991); *Talking from Nine to Five* (1995); *The Argument Culture: Moving From Debate to Dialogue* (1998); and *The Argument: Stopping America's War of Words* (1999).

BEFORE YOU READ

PREREADING
DISCUSSION

1. Do you like talk shows? Daytime talk shows tend to be somewhat serious, and nighttime talk shows tend to be more humorous. Which talk shows do you watch and/or prefer?

2. What kinds of TV shows do you like best?

3. Have you ever watched *The Oprah Winfrey Show*? What is your opinion of the show?

● ●

The TV Host: Oprah Winfrey

She didn't create the talk-show format.
But the compassion and intimacy she put into it have created a new way for us
to talk to one another.

By Deborah Tannen

1   The Sudanese-born supermodel Alek Wek stands poised and insouciant as the talk-show host, admiring her classic African features, cradles Wek's cheek and says, "What a difference it would have made to my childhood if I had seen someone who looks like you on television." The host is Oprah Winfrey, and she has been making that difference for millions of viewers, young and old, black and white, for nearly a dozen years.

2   Winfrey stands as a beacon, not only in the worlds of media and entertainment but also in the larger realm of public discourse. At 44, she has a

*hot caring/
worrying*

163

personal fortune estimated at more than half a billion dollars. She owns her own production company, which creates feature films, prime-time TV specials and home videos. An accomplished actress, she won an Academy Award nomination for her role in *The Color Purple*, and this fall will star in her own film production of Toni Morrison's *Beloved*.

3   But it is through her talk show that her influence has been greatest. When Winfrey talks, her viewers—an estimated 14 million daily in the U.S. and millions more in 132 other countries—listen. Any book she chooses for her on-air book club becomes an instant best seller. When she established the "world's largest piggy bank," people all over the country contributed spare change to raise more than $1 million (matched by Oprah) to send disadvantaged kids to college. When she blurted that hearing about the threat of mad-cow disease "just stopped me cold from eating another burger!", the perceived threat to the beef industry was enough to trigger a multimillion-dollar lawsuit (which she won).

4   Born in 1954 to unmarried parents, Winfrey was raised by her grandmother on a farm with no indoor plumbing in Kosciusko, Miss. By age 3 she was reading the Bible and reciting in church. At 6 she moved to her mother's home in Milwaukee, Wis.; later, to her father's in Nashville, Tenn. A lonely child, she found solace in books. When a seventh-grade teacher noticed

the young girl reading during lunch, he got her a scholarship to a better school. Winfrey's talent for public performance and spontaneity in answering questions helped her win beauty contests—and get her first taste of public attention.

5   Crowned Miss Fire Prevention in Nashville at 17, Winfrey visited a local radio station, where she was invited to read copy for a lark—and was hired to read news on the air. Two years later, while a sophomore at Tennessee State University, she was hired as Nashville's first female and first black TV-news anchor. After graduation, she took an anchor position in Baltimore, Md., but lacked the detachment to be a reporter. She cried when a story was sad, laughed when she misread a word. Instead, she was given an early-morning talk show. She had found her medium. In 1984 she moved on to be the host of *A.M. Chicago*, which became *The Oprah Winfrey Show*. It was syndicated in 1986—when Winfrey was 32—and soon overtook *Donahue* as the nation's top-rated talk show.

6   Women, especially, listen to Winfrey because they feel as if she's a friend. Although Phil Donahue pioneered the format she uses (mike-holding host moves among an audience whose members question guests), his show was mostly what I call "report-talk," which often typifies men's conversation. The overt focus is on information. Winfrey transformed the format into what I call "rapport-talk," the

---

B ORN Jan. 29, 1954, in Kosciusko, Miss.
1971 Competes in Miss Black America pageant
1973 First black and first woman hired to anchor TV news in Nashville, Tenn.
1977 Starts co-hosting *People Are Talking* morning show in Baltimore, Md.
1986 *The Oprah Winfrey Show* goes national; Oscar-nominated for *The Color Purple*
1996 Launches book club
1998 Produces, stars in Toni Morrison's *Beloved*

back-and-forth conversation that is the basis of female friendship, with its emphasis on self-revealing intimacies. She turned the focus from experts to ordinary people talking about personal issues. Girls' and women's friendships are often built on trading secrets. Winfrey's power is that she tells her own, divulging that she once ate a package of hot-dog buns drenched in maple syrup, that she had smoked cocaine, even that she had been raped as a child. With Winfrey, the talk show became more immediate, more confessional, more personal. When a guest's story moves her, she cries and spreads her arms for a hug.

> "More than a great star, you are a 20th century political figure. Your good works have touched all of us."
>
> PHIL DONAHUE, when Oprah received an Emmy for Lifetime Achievement

7   When my book *You Just Don't Understand: Women and Men in Conversation* was published, I was lucky enough to appear on both *Donahue* and *Oprah*—and to glimpse the difference between them. Winfrey related my book to her own life: she began by saying she had read the book and "saw myself over and over" in it. She then told one of my examples, adding, "I've done that a thousand times"—and illustrated it by describing herself and Stedman. (Like close friends, viewers know her "steady beau" by first name.)

8   Winfrey saw television's power to blend public and private; while it links strangers and conveys information over public airwaves, TV is most often viewed in the privacy of our homes. Like a family member, it sits down to meals with us and talks to us in the lonely afternoons. Grasping this paradox, Oprah exhorts viewers to improve their lives and the world. She makes people care because she cares. That is Winfrey's genius, and will be her legacy, as the changes she has wrought in the talk show continue to permeate our culture and shape our lives.

> "I used to speak in the church all the time, and the sisters in the front row would say to my grandmother, "Hattie Mae, this child sure can talk."—Oprah Winfrey

HOW WELL DID YOU READ?

A. Circle the letter of the choice that best completes the sentence or answers the question.

1. The article mainly discusses _____ .

   a. Oprah's childhood
   b. the history of *The Oprah Winfrey Show*
   c. how Oprah has become such an influential TV personality
   d. the differences between Oprah Winfrey and Phil Donahue

2. The tone of this article can best be described as _____ .

    a. detached
    b. admiring   ← Why? Words?
    c. forgiving
    d. insulting

3. According to the author, Oprah's influence has been the greatest _____ .

    a. through her talk show
    b. as a movie actress
    c. in her legal battles
    d. through her production company

4. Where does the author contrast the way that men and women relate to each other?

    a. paragraph 5
    b. paragraph 6
    c. paragraph 7
    d. paragraph 8

5. Which of the following is not discussed in the article?

    a. the author's appearance on *The Oprah Winfrey Show*
    b. why Oprah was not meant to be a reporter
    c. why women listen to Oprah
    d. what Oprah plans to do in the future

6. The author supports which of the following conclusions?

    a. Oprah has changed the nature and impact of talk shows.
    b. Oprah's emphasis on information is the key to her success.
    c. Oprah's production company will be her legacy.
    d. none of the above

B. Make a list of Oprah's accomplishments.

_____

_____

_____

_____

_____

**BUILDING
READING SKILLS**

MAKING
INFERENCES

Read the following statements. Put a check mark next to the statements you can infer from information in the article.

_____ 1. Oprah has a lot of influence on her audience's choice of books to read.

_____ 2. Talk-show hosts do not need to be detached from the issues discussed on their shows.

_____ 3. Oprah believes that a college education is important.

_____ 4. Oprah's grandmother didn't have a lot of money.

_____ 5. Oprah likes all the guests she has on her show.

_____ 6. Oprah always wanted to be a talk-show host.

_____ 7. Men and women have different styles of talking.

_____ 8. Oprah always wins lawsuits that are brought against her.

_____ 9. Women make better talk show hosts than men.

EXPANDING VOCABULARY

Using a dictionary, write the part of speech for each word, the meaning as it is used in the article, any synonyms for the word, and a sentence to help you remember the meaning. For the last three items, choose words from the article that were unfamiliar to you.

1. accomplished (¶2)

part of speech: _____

definition: _____

synonyms: _____

sentence: _____

_____

2. influence (¶3)

part of speech: _____

definition: _____

synonyms: _____

sentence: _____

_____

3. contribute (¶3)

part of speech: _____

definition: _____

synonyms: _____

sentence: _____

_____

4. spontaneity (¶4)

part of speech: _____

definition: _____

synonyms: _____

sentence: _____

_____

5. detachment (¶5)

part of speech: _____

definition: _____

synonyms: _____

sentence: _____

_____

6. move (¶6)

part of speech: _____

definition: _____

synonyms: _____

sentence: _____

_____

7. exhort (¶8)

part of speech: _____

definition: _____

synonyms: _____

sentence: _____

_____

8. _____ (¶   )

part of speech: _____

definition: _____

synonyms: _____

sentence: _____

_____

9. _____ (¶   )

part of speech: _____

definition: _____

synonyms: _____

sentence: _____

_____

10. _____ (¶   )

part of speech: _____

definition: _____

synonyms: _____

sentence: _____

_____

BUILDING READING SKILLS

UNDERSTANDING REFERENCES

Write the word or phrase that the highlighted reference refers to.

1. _She owns her own production company, **which** creates feature films, prime-time TV specials and home videos._

   which = _____

2. _When she blurted that hearing about the threat of mad-cow disease "just stopped me cold from eating another burger!", the perceived threat to the beef industry was enough to trigger a multimillion-dollar lawsuit (**which** she won)._

   which = _____

3. _Crowned Miss Fire Prevention in Nashville at 17, Winfrey visited a local radio station, **where** she was invited to read copy for a lark—and was hired to read news on the air._

   where = _____

4. _In 1984 she moved on to be the host of A.M. Chicago, **which** became The Oprah Winfrey Show. **It** was syndicated in 1986—when Winfrey was 32—and soon overtook Donahue as the nation's top-rated talk show._

   which = _____

   it = _____

5. *Women, especially, listen to Winfrey because **they** feel as if she's a friend. Although Phil Donahue pioneered the format **she** uses (mike-holding host moves among an audience **whose members** question guests), his show was mostly what I call "report-talk," **which** often typifies men's conversation.*

they = _____

she = _____

whose members = _____

which = _____

6. *Winfrey transformed the format into what I call "rapport-talk," the back-and-forth conversation **that** is the basis of female friendship, with **its** emphasis on self-revealing intimacies.*

both same

that = _____

its = _____

7. *Girls' and women's friendships are often built on trading secrets. Winfrey's power is that she tells **her own** . . .*

her own = _____

8. *When my book* You Just Don't Understand: Women and Men in Conversation *was published, I was lucky enough to appear on both* Donahue *and* Oprah—*and to glimpse the difference between **them**.*

them = _____

9. *Winfrey saw television's power to blend public and private; while **it** links strangers and conveys information over public airwaves, TV is most often viewed in the privacy of our homes. Like a family member, **it** sits down to meals with us and talks to us in the lonely afternoons.*

it = _____

it = _____

10. *She makes people care because she cares. **That** is Winfrey's genius, and will be her legacy, as the changes she has wrought in the talk show continue to permeate our culture and shape our lives.*

that = _____

RESPOND IN WRITING

Watch an *Oprah* show. Write a letter to Oprah in which you agree or disagree with some point that was made in the show.

_____

_____

_____

_____

_____

_____

_____

_____

_____

_____

_____

_____

_____

_____

_____

_____

_____

_____

_____

_____

_____

_____

_____

_____

_____

_____

_____

_____

_____

Lucille Ball is generally considered the greatest comedienne of all time. As the following article "The TV Star: Lucille Ball" shows, there is little question that she is the most loved television comedienne in history. For more than five decades, people around the world have tuned in to *I Love Lucy* to watch her portrayal of a scatterbrained housewife.

1. Who are your favorite comedians?

2. Have you ever watched *I Love Lucy*? Which episode is your favorite?

3. What do you like best or least about Lucy?

The TV Star: Lucille Ball

The first lady of comedy brought us laughter as well as emotional truth. No wonder everybody loved Lucy.

By Richard Zoglin

I Love Lucy is the most consistently popular TV show in history.

1   *I Love Lucy* debuted on CBS in October 1951, but at first it looked little different from other domestic comedies that were starting to make the move from radio to TV, like *My Favorite Husband*, the radio show Ball had co-starred in for three years. Lucy Ricardo was, in those early *I Love Lucy* episodes, just a generic daffy housewife. Ethel (Vivian Vance), her neighbor and landlady, was a stock busybody. Desi Arnaz, as bandleader Ricky Ricardo, hadn't yet become one of the finest straight men in TV history. William Frawley, as Fred Mertz, seemed a Hollywood has-been in search of work, which he was.

2   Then magic struck. Guided by Ball's comic brilliance, the show developed the shape and depth of great comedy. Lucy's quirks and foibles—her craving to be in show biz, her crazy schemes that always backfired, the constant fights with the Mertzes—became as particularized and familiar as the face across the dinner table. For four out of its six seasons (only six!), *I Love Lucy* was the No. 1–rated show on television; at its peak, in 1952-53, it averaged an incredible 67.3 rating, meaning that on a typical Monday night, more than two-thirds of all homes with TV sets were tuned to *Lucy*.

3   Ball's dizzy redhead with the elastic face and saucer eyes was the model for scores of comic TV females to follow. She and her show, moreover,

B ORN Aug. 6, 1911, in Jamestown, N.Y.
1933 Moves to Hollywood
1937 Stars in *Stage Door* with Katharine Hepburn
1940 Marries Desi Arnaz
1951 *I Love Lucy* premieres on CBS
1953 The birth of Little Ricky becomes a national media event
1960 Divorces Arnaz
1962 Buys Arnaz's share of Desilu Productions and becomes first woman to head a major studio
1989 Dies April 26 in Los Angeles

more distinctive look, turned it red in 1942), she landed bit parts in B movies and moved up to classy fare like *Stage Door,* in which she held her own with Katharine Hepburn and Ginger Rogers.

5 Buster Keaton, the great silent clown working as a consultant at MGM, recognized her comic gifts and worked with her on stunts. She got a few chances to show off her talent in films like *DuBarry Was a Lady* (with Red Skelton) and *Fancy Pants* (with Bob Hope) but never broke through to the top. By the end of the 1940s, with Ball approaching 40, her movie career was all but finished.

6 It was her husband Desi—a Cuban bandleader she married shortly after they met on the set of *Too Many Girls* in 1940—who urged her to try television. CBS was interested in Ball, but not in the fellow with the pronounced Spanish accent she wanted to play her husband. To prove that the audience would accept them as a couple, Lucy and Desi cooked up a vaudeville act and took it on tour. It got rave reviews ("a sock new act," said *Variety*), and CBS relented.

7 But there were other haggles. Lucy and Desi wanted to shoot the show in Hollywood, rather than in New York City, where most TV was then being done. And for better quality, they insisted on shooting on film, rather than doing it live and recording on kinescope. CBS balked at the extra cost; the couple agreed to take a salary cut in return for full ownership of the program. It was a shrewd business decision: *I Love Lucy* was the launching pad for Desilu Productions, which (with other shows, like *Our Miss Brooks* and *The Untouchables*) became one of TV's most successful independent producers, before Paramount bought it in 1967.

helped define a still nascent medium. Before *I Love Lucy,* TV was feeling its way, adapting forms from other media. Live TV drama was an outgrowth of Broadway theater; game shows were transplanted from radio; variety shows and early comedy stars like Milton Berle came out of vaudeville. *I Love Lucy* was unmistakably a television show, and Ball the perfect star for the small screen. "I look like everybody's idea of an actress," she once said, "but I feel like a housewife." Sid Caesar and Jackie Gleason were big men with larger-than-life personas: Lucy was one of us.

4 She grew up in Jamestown, N.Y., where her father, an electrician, died when she was just three. At 15 she began making forays to New York City to try to break into show business. She had little luck as an actress but worked as a model before moving to Hollywood in 1933 for a part in the chorus of *Roman Scandals.* Strikingly pretty, with chestnut hair dyed blond (until MGM hairdressers, seeking a

"Anybody alive who had TV felt Lucy was part of the family. I don't know if that ever will be duplicated."

CAROL BURNETT, at the time of
Ball's death in 1989

8   Today *I Love Lucy*, with its farcical plots, broad physical humor and unliberated picture of marriage, is sometimes dismissed as a relic. Yet the show has the timeless perfection of a crystal goblet. For all its comic hyperbole, *Lucy* explored universal themes: the tensions of married life, the clash between career and home, the meaning of loyalty and friendship. The series also reflected most of the decade's important social trends. The Ricardos made their contribution to the baby boom in January 1953—TV's Little Ricky was born on the same day that Ball gave birth, by caesarean, to her second child, Desi Jr. (A daughter, Lucie, had been born in 1951.) They traveled to California just as the nation was turning west, in a hilarious series of shows that epitomized our conception of—and obsession with—Hollywood glamour. And when the nation began moving to the suburbs, so too, in their last season, did the Ricardos.

9   Ball was a lithe and inventive physical comedian, and her famous slapstick bits—trying to keep up with a candy assembly line, stomping grapes in an Italian wine vat—were justly celebrated. But she was far more than a clown. Her mobile face could register a whole dictionary of emotions; her comic timing was unmatched; her devotion to the truth of her character never flagged. She was a tireless perfectionist. For one scene in which she needed to pop a paper bag, she spent three hours testing bags to make sure she got the right size and sound.

10   Most of all, *I Love Lucy* was grounded in emotional honesty. Though the couple had a tempestuous marriage off-screen (Desi was an unrepentant philanderer), the Ricardos' kisses showed the spark of real attraction. In the episode where Lucy finds out she is pregnant, she can't break the news to Ricky because he is too busy. Finally, she takes a table at his nightclub show and passes him an anonymous note asking that he sing a song, *We're Having a Baby*, to the father-to-be. As Ricky roams the room looking for the happy couple, he spies Lucy and moves on. Then he does a heartrending double take, glides to his knees and asks, voice cracking, whether it's true. Finishing the scene together onstage, the couple are overcome by the real emotion of their own impending baby. Director William Asher, dismayed by the unrehearsed tears, even shot a second, more upbeat take. Luckily he used the first one; it's the most touching moment in sitcom history.

11   Tired of the grind of a weekly series, Lucy and Desi ended *I Love Lucy* in 1957, when it was still No. 1. For three more years, they did hourlong specials, then broke up the act for good when they divorced in 1960. Ball returned to TV with two other popular (if less satisfying) TV series, *The Lucy Show* and *Here's Lucy;* made a few more movies (starring in *Mame* in 1974); and attempted a final comeback in the 1986 ABC sitcom *Life with Lucy*, which lasted an ignominious eight weeks. But *I Love Lucy* lives on in reruns around the world, an endless loop of laughter and a reminder of the woman who helped make TV a habit, and an art.

HOW WELL DID YOU READ?

EXAMPLES

List the examples that the author uses to support each of the following points.

1. Although *I Love Lucy* was a comedy show, it explored universal themes.

    a. _tensions of married life_
    b. _clash between career and home_
    c. _meaning of loyalty and friendship_

2. Lucy had several famous slapstick skits.

    a. _trying to keep up with a candy assembly line_
    b. _crushing grapes in an Italian wine vat_
    c. _____

3. But she was far more than a clown.

    a. _her face could register so many emotions_
    b. _comic timing_
    c. _devotion to her 'character's' truth_

4. Lucy was a tireless perfectionist.

    a. _Spent hours testing bags to make sure_
    b. _the skit would work properly_
    c. _____

5. Desi and Lucy had to overcome several obstacles in order to get the show to be just the way they wanted it.

    a. _CBS wanted Lucy, not Desi_
    b. _Wanted to shoot in Hollywood, not NYC_
    c. _Insisted on using film, not kinescope_

eccentricities

6. Lucy's quirks and foibles became familiar to her audience.

    a. _Craving to be in show biz_
    b. _Crazy schemes always backfire_
    c. _Constant fights with Mertzes_

175

Read the following sentences and underline the transitions. Write the transition word(s) on the line and identify the type of relationship signified. Review the chart on pages 147–148 if you need to.

1. I Love Lucy *debuted on CBS in October 1951, but at first it looked little different from other domestic comedies that were starting to make the move from radio to TV . . .*

   Transition: _____ but _____

   Type of relationship: _____ contrast _____

2. *Ball's dizzy redhead with the elastic face and saucer eyes was the model for scores of comic TV females to follow. She and her show, moreover, helped define a still nascent medium.*

   Transition: _____ moreover _____

   Type of relationship: _____ addition _____

3. *Before* I Love Lucy, *TV was feeling its way, adapting forms from other media.*

   Transition: _____ before _____

   Type of relationship: _____ time _____

4. *. . . variety shows and early comedy stars like Milton Berle came out of vaudeville.*

   Transition: _____ like _____

   Type of relationship: _____ Illustration / example _____

5. *"I look like everybody's idea of an actress," she once said, "but I feel like a housewife."*

   Transition: _____ but _____

   Type of relationship: _____ contrast _____

6. *Strikingly pretty, with chestnut hair dyed blond (until MGM hairdressers, seeking a more distinctive look, turned it red in 1942), she landed bit parts in B movies and moved up to classy fare like* Stage Door *. . .*

   Transition: _____ until _____

   Type of relationship: _____ time _____

7. *Lucy and Desi wanted to shoot the show in Hollywood, rather than in New York City, where most TV was then being done.*

   Transition: _____ rather than _____

   Type of relationship: _____ contrast _____

8. *Today* I Love Lucy, *with its farcical plots, broad physical humor and unliberated picture of marriage, is sometimes dismissed as a relic. Yet the show has the timeless perfection of a crystal goblet.*

   Transition: _____ *Yet* _____

   Type of relationship: _____ *contrast* _____

9. *The series also reflected most of the decade's important social trends.*

   Transition: _____ *also* _____

   Type of relationship: _____ *addition* _____

10. *They traveled to California just as the nation was turning west, in a hilarious series of shows that epitomized our conception of—and obsession with—Hollywood glamour.*

    Transition: _____ *just as* _____

    Type of relationship: _____ *time* _____

11. *Though the couple had a tempestuous marriage off-screen (Desi was an unrepentant philanderer), the Ricardos' kisses showed the spark of real attraction.*

    Transition: _____ *though* _____

    Type of relationship: _____ *concession* _____

EXPANDING VOCABULARY

Using a dictionary, write the part of speech for each word, the meaning as it is used in the article, any synonyms for the word, and a sentence to help you remember the meaning. For the last three items, choose words from the article that were unfamiliar to you.

1. brilliance (¶2)

   part of speech: _____

   definition: _____

   synonyms: _____

   sentence: _____

   _____

2. craving (¶2)

part of speech: _____

definition: _____

synonyms: _____

sentence: _____

_____

3. shrewd (¶7)

part of speech: _____

definition: _____

synonyms: _____

sentence: _____

_____

4. perfection (¶8)

part of speech: _____

definition: _____

synonyms: _____

sentence: _____

_____

5. hilarious (¶8)

part of speech: _____

definition: _____

synonyms: _____

sentence: _____

_____

6. devotion (¶9)

part of speech: _____

definition: _____

synonyms: _____

sentence: _____

_____

7. episode (¶10)

   part of speech: _____

   definition: _____

   synonyms: _____

   sentence: _____

   _____

8. _____ (¶   )

   part of speech: _____

   definition: _____

   synonyms: _____

   sentence: _____

   _____

9. _____ (¶   )

   part of speech: _____

   definition: _____

   synonyms: _____

   sentence: _____

   _____

10. _____ (¶   )

   part of speech: _____

   definition: _____

   synonyms: _____

   sentence: _____

   _____

**BUILDING
READING SKILLS**

FACT VERSUS
OPINION

Read the following statements. If a statement is a fact, write *FACT* on the
line. If a statement is an opinion, write *OPINION* on the line.

_____F_____ 1. *I Love Lucy* was rated No. 1 for four out of its six seasons on TV.

_____O_____ 2. The scene where Lucy tells Ricky that she is pregnant is the
most touching moment in TV sitcom history.

_____O_____ 3. *I Love Lucy* has the timeless perfection of a crystal goblet.

_____F_____ 4. Paramount bought Desilu Productions in 1967.

_____O_____ 5. Desi Arnaz was one of the best straight men in the history of TV.

**BUILDING
WRITING SKILLS**

PARAPHRASING

Paraphrase the following passages. Your paraphrase should express the
main idea of the original passage as clearly and simply as possible.

1. I Love Lucy *debuted on CBS in October 1951, but at first it looked little different
from other domestic comedies that were starting to make the move from radio to TV,
like* My Favorite Husband, *the radio show Ball had co-starred in for three years.*

_____

_____

_____

2. *Today* I Love Lucy, *with its farcical plots, broad physical humor and unliberated
picture of marriage, is sometimes dismissed as a relic. Yet the show has the timeless
perfection of a crystal goblet.*

_____

_____

_____

3. *They traveled to California just as the nation was turning west, in a hilarious series
of shows that epitomized our conception of—and obsession with—Hollywood glamour. And when the nation began moving to the suburbs, so too, in their last season,
did the Ricardos.*

_____

_____

_____

_____

TALK IT OVER

DISCUSSION

What qualities do you think both Oprah and Lucy have that helped make them such successful TV personalities?

RESPOND IN WRITING

A. Reread the two articles again, looking for comparisons between Oprah Winfrey and Lucille Ball. Make a list of three important similarities between the two women.

1. _____

2. _____

3. _____

Use your list as a guide to write a paragraph on a separate piece of paper, comparing Oprah Winfrey and Lucille Ball. Add details to support your points.

B. Watch an episode of the *I Love Lucy* show. On a separate piece of paper, write about your reaction to the episode. You should include a summary of the show, a short description of the parts you found the funniest, and the universal theme that the episode explored.

BUILDING READING SKILLS

INCREASING READING SPEED

You will have 20 seconds to underline the word that is the same as the first word in each line.

1. well	we'll	well	weld	welt	low
2. pen	pen	pin	pan	pens	send
3. up	at	in	up	pup	pull
4. use	union	sue	use	under	seven
5. ever	even	every	under	ever	never
6. tidy	tie	untie	tidy	tin	tan
7. suit	soup	sun	tile	suit	see
8. tea	tee	ten	tea	ate	ache
9. orange	over	range	round	orange	angel
10. egg	leg	get	eggs	exact	egg
11. box	sox	fox	talks	box	boxes
12. gag	gaggle	bag	big	fig	gag
13. boat	bone	boat	bog	boot	bloke
14. put	poor	fun	push	put	pant
15. still	style	tile	stilt	until	still

When you have finished, figure out how many answers you got right and check the appropriate box on page 263 in order to keep track of your progress.

People of all ages know and love Jim Henson's Muppets. They demonstrate well the astounding range of his creative imagination. Meant for the young and the young at heart, Henson's puppets have charmed and captivated audiences since the 1950s, as discussed in the following article, "The TV Creator: Jim Henson."

1. Have you ever seen any of the Muppet movies? Which ones?

2. Which Muppets do you like best? Why?

3. What words would you use to describe the Muppets?

4. Why do you think Jim Henson's Muppets have captured the hearts of so many people all over the world?

The TV Creator: Jim Henson

Hundreds of millions of kids—and adults—have been
entranced by the Muppetmaster

By James Collins

1   Jim Henson can be credited with many accomplishments: he had the most profound influence on children of any entertainer of his time; he adapted the ancient art of puppetry to the most modern of mediums, television, transforming both; he created a TV show that was one of the most popular on earth. But Henson's greatest achievement was broader than any of these. Through his work, he helped sustain the qualities of fancifulness, warmth and consideration that have been so threatened by our coarse, cynical age.

2   Born in 1936, Henson grew up in the small town of Leland, Miss., where his father worked as an agronomist for the Federal Government. When Henson was in fifth grade, his father took a job in Washington, and the family moved to a suburb in Maryland. There, in high school, Henson became fascinated by television. "I loved the idea," he once said, "that what you saw was taking place somewhere else at the same time." In the summer of 1954, just before he entered the University of Maryland, he learned that a local

station needed someone to perform with puppets on a children's show. Henson wasn't particularly interested in puppets, but he did want to get into TV, so he and a friend made a couple—one was called Pierre the French Rat—and they were hired.

3 The job didn't last long, but within a few months, Henson was back on TV, puppeteering for another station, the local NBC affiliate. Soon he had his own five-minute program, called *Sam and Friends*. It aired live twice a day, once before the network news with Chet Huntley and David Brinkley and later preceding the *Tonight* show, which at that time starred Steve Allen. Remaining in college, where he studied art and theater design, Henson produced *Sam and Friends* for six years. Assisting him was a fellow student named Jane Nebel, whom he married in 1959.

4 Puppets have been around for thousands of years, but the proto-Muppets that began to appear on *Sam and Friends* were different. Kermit was there, looking and sounding much as he would later (until his death Henson always animated Kermit and provided his voice). Typical hand puppets have solid heads, but Kermit's face was soft and mobile, and he could move his mouth in synchronization with his speech; he could also gesticulate more facilely than a marionette, with rods moving his arms. For television, Henson realized, it was necessary to invent puppets that had "life and

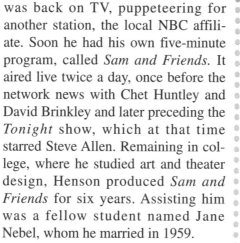

sensitivity." (Henson sometimes said *Muppet* was a combination of *puppet* and *marionette*, but it seems the word came to him and he liked it, and later thought up a derivation.)

5 Throughout the early 1960s, the Muppets made appearances on the *Today* show and a range of variety programs. Then, in 1969, came *Sesame Street*. Henson was always careful not to take the credit for *Sesame Street*'s achievements. It was not his program, after all—the Children's Television Workshop hired him. In fact, Henson hesitated to join the show, since he did not want to become stuck as a children's entertainer. Nonetheless, few would disagree that it was primarily Bert and Ernie, Big Bird, Grover and the rest who made *Sesame Street* so captivating. Joan Ganz Cooney, who created the show, once remarked that the group involved with it had a collective genius but that Henson was the only individual genius. "He was our era's Charlie Chaplin, Mae West, W.C. Fields and Marx Brothers," Cooney said, "and indeed he drew from all of them to create a new art form that influenced popular culture around the world."

"He was one of the world's greatest positive thinkers . . . My father had the ability to make the good guy the more interesting, crazy, eccentric character."

BRIAN HENSON, son

BORN Sept. 24, 1936, in Greenville, Miss.
1954 Gets first TV job as a puppeteer on a local Maryland station
1955 Creates Kermit, his alter ego.
1959 Marries Jane Nebel
1969 *Sesame Street* appears on PBS, introducing Bert, Ernie, and Big Bird
1976 Launches *The Muppet Show*, starring Kermit and Miss Piggy
1990 Dies suddenly in New York City on May 16

⁶ Since *Sesame Street* has been on the air for 30 years and has been shown in scores of countries, Henson's Muppets have entranced hundreds of millions of children. And the audience for the Muppets has not only been huge; it has also been passionate. In fact, given the number of his fans and the intensity of their devotion, Kermit may possibly be the leading children's character of the century, more significant than even Peter Pan or Winnie-the-Pooh.

⁷ But despite the Muppets' success on *Sesame Street* and their demonstrated appeal to adults as well as children, no U.S. network would give Henson a show of his own. It was a British producer, Lew Grade, who finally offered Henson the financing that enabled him to mount *The Muppet Show*. The program ran in syndication from 1976 until 1981, when Henson decided to end it lest its quality begin to decline. At its peak it was watched each week by 235 million viewers around the world. Stars from Steve Martin to Rudolf Nureyev appeared as guest hosts, and the show launched the career of Miss Piggy, the vain, *trés sophistiquée* female who was besotted with Kermit.

⁸ The beauty of the Muppets, on both *Sesame Street* and their own show, was that they were cuddly but not too cuddly, and not only cuddly. There are satire and sly wit; Bert and Ernie quarrel; Miss Piggy behaves unbecomingly; Kermit is sometimes exasperated. By adding just enough tartness to a sweet overall spirit, Henson purveyed a kind of innocence that was plausible for the modern imagination. His knowingness allowed us to accept his real gifts: wonder, delight, optimism.

⁹ Henson was a kind, infinitely patient man. Those who worked for him say he literally never raised his voice. Frank

Oz, the puppeteer behind Bert, Miss Piggy and many others, was Henson's partner for 27 years. "Jim was not perfect," he says. "But I'll tell you something—he was as close to how you're supposed to behave toward other people as anyone I've ever known."

¹⁰ The only complaint of his five children seems to be that because Henson was so busy, he was unable to spend enough time with them. They often accompanied him while he worked, and he once even took his eldest daughter along when he held a meeting with the head of a movie studio. That child, Lisa, is now a powerful producer in Hollywood; Henson's elder son Brian runs the Jim Henson Co.; and another daughter, Cheryl, also works there. However gentle, Henson was not a complete naif. He liked expensive cars—Rolls-Royces, Porsches—and after he and Jane separated in 1986 (they remained close and never divorced), he dated a succession of women.

¹¹ In the '70s and '80s, Henson produced innumerable films and TV shows with and without the Muppets. Some were dark, like his adaptations of folktales and myths in the ingenious TV series *Jim Henson's The Storyteller.* Then in 1990, at age 53, Henson suddenly died after contracting an extremely aggressive form of pneumonia. He remains a powerful presence, though, on account of *Sesame Street* and the Henson Co., whose next venture will be a global family-entertainment network called the Kermit Channel. Because the works we encounter as children are so potent, Henson may influence the next century as much as this one, as his viewers grow up carrying his vision within them.

FYI

Kermit the Frog got an honorary doctorate in "amphibious letters" in 1996 from Southampton College on Long Island, New York. Kermit accepted his degree "personally," with the help of Muppeteer Steve Whitmire.

A. Using paragraph numbers in the article, identify the paragraph(s) that

_____ 1. describe(s) the difference between typical hand puppets and Muppets.

_____ 2. discuss(es) Henson's contribution to _Sesame Street_.

_____ 3. give(s) information about _The Muppet Show_.

_____ 4. list(s) Henson's accomplishments.

_____ 5. explain(s) the appeal of the Muppets.

_____ 6. tell(s) about Henson's childhood.

_____ 7. describe(s) what Henson's children do.

B. Answer the following questions.

1. According to the author, what are Henson's accomplishments?

   a. _____

   b. _____

   c. _____

2. What is his greatest achievement?

   _____

3. In your own words, explain the appeal of the Muppets.

   _____

   _____

   _____

Using a dictionary, write the part of speech for each word, the meaning as it is used in the article, any synonyms for the word, and a sentence to help you remember the meaning. For the last three items, choose words from the article that were unfamiliar to you.

1. ancient (¶1)

   part of speech: _____

   definition: _____

   synonyms: _____

   sentence: _____

   _____

2. achievement (¶1)

part of speech: _____

definition: _____

synonyms: _____

sentence: _____

_____

3. hesitate (¶5)

part of speech: _____

definition: _____

synonyms: _____

sentence: _____

_____

4. primarily (¶5)

part of speech: _____

definition: _____

synonyms: _____

sentence: _____

_____

5. intensity (¶6)

part of speech: _____

definition: _____

synonyms: _____

sentence: _____

_____

6. patient (¶9)

part of speech: _____

definition: _____

synonyms: _____

sentence: _____

_____

7. potent (¶11)

part of speech: _____

definition: _____

synonyms: _____

sentence: _____

_____

8. _____ (¶   )

part of speech: _____

definition: _____

synonyms: _____

sentence: _____

_____

9. _____ (¶   )

part of speech: _____

definition: _____

synonyms: _____

sentence: _____

_____

10. _____ (¶   )

part of speech: _____

definition: _____

synonyms: _____

sentence: _____

_____

BUILDING WRITING SKILLS

PARAPHRASING

Paraphrase the following passages. Your paraphrase should express the main idea of the original passage as clearly and simply as possible.

1. *But despite the Muppets' success on* Sesame Street *and their demonstrated appeal to adults as well as children, no U.S. network would give Henson a show of his own.*

_____

_____

_____

2. *Because the works we encounter as children are so potent, Henson may influence the next century as much as this one, as his viewers grow up carrying his vision within them.*

_____

_____

_____

3. *Since* Sesame Street *has been on the air for 30 years and has been shown in scores of countries, Henson's Muppets have entranced hundreds of millions of children. And the audience for the Muppets has not only been huge; it has also been passionate.*

_____

_____

_____

BUILDING WRITING SKILLS

UNDERSTANDING REFERENCES

Write the word or phrase that the highlighted reference refers to.

1. *Henson wasn't particularly interested in puppets, but . . . he and a friend made **a couple**—one was called Pierre the French Rat—and they were hired.*

a couple = _____

2. *. . . he adapted the ancient art of puppetry to the most modern of mediums, television, transforming **both** . . .*

both = _____

3. *Henson sometimes said* Muppet *was a combination of* puppet *and* marionette, *but it seems **the word** came to him and he liked it, and later thought up a derivation.*

the word = _____

4. *Then, in 1969, came* Sesame Street. *Henson was always careful not to take credit for* Sesame Street's *achievements.* **It** *was not his program, after all—the Children's Television workshop hired him.*

   It = _____

5. *It was a British producer, Lew Grade, who finally offered Henson the financing that enabled him to mount* The Muppet Show. **The program** *ran in syndication from 1976 until 1981, when Henson decided to end it lest its quality begin to decline.*

   The program = _____

RESPOND IN WRITING

Using the articles in this unit, write an essay about the influence that TV personalities such as Lucille Ball, Jim Henson, and Oprah Winfrey have on our lives. You should include an introduction, three main paragraphs, and a conclusion. Use the following sentence as your thesis statement:

Three influential television personalities who have influenced our lives are Lucille Ball, the first lady of comedy who brought laughter and emotional truth to TV audiences all over the world; Oprah Winfrey, the talk-show host who brought compassion and intimacy to TV; and Jim Henson, a performing genius who brought enjoyment to hundreds of millions of children and adults.

BUILDING WRITING SKILLS

USING QUOTATIONS

After you have finished your first draft, think about whether or not there are places in your essay where quotations from the original articles would be helpful in supporting the ideas you are discussing. You should use a quote only if the exact words of the author are so precise and exceptionally well stated that you feel it is necessary to quote them in order to get your point across clearly. In other cases, you can simply paraphrase.

If you decide to quote the exact words of the author, you will need to use an appropriate method to introduce the quotation and you will need to punctuate it appropriately.

INTRODUCING A QUOTATION

In an essay or research paper, a quotation is always introduced. Some of the expressions commonly used to introduce a quotation include:

According to _____

As _____ said

I agree/disagree with _____'s view that

_____ states that

_____ points out that

USING
QUOTATION
MARKS

The rules that govern the punctuation of quotations in essays and research papers are as follows:

Put the speaker's exact words inside quotation marks.

A comma separates the quotation from the rest of the sentence.

Capitalize the first word of the quote.

Put periods, commas, or question marks inside the final quotation marks.

Example: As my mother said, "Lucille Ball is the funniest person who has ever been on TV."

USING ELLIPSIS

You will find that sometimes you only want to quote part of what someone has said. In such cases, use three dots to indicate that some of the original quote has been omitted. This is called **ellipsis.**

Example: According to Richard Zoglin, "Lucy's quirks and foibles . . . became as particularized and familiar as the face across the dinner table."

USING BRACKETS

Sometimes you may need to add or change a word for the quote to read smoothly. This is especially true if you have omitted words from the original. If you add or change words, put the new words in brackets.

Example: According to Richard Zoglin, "Guided by Ball's comic brilliance, [*I Love Lucy*] developed the shape and depth of great comedy."

AVOIDING
PLAGIARISM

Plagiarism involves copying someone else's words and/or ideas and pretending that they are your own. Plagiarism is illegal and an extremely serious offense. Whenever you use someone else's words, either by quoting directly or by paraphrasing, it is very important to both acknowledge the author by stating his or her name (if available) and identify the source of the quote.

ORAL REPORT

Research one of the following entertainers. Look for information about his or her childhood, significant achievements, and influence on society. Prepare a five-minute oral presentation for your class.

Ed Sullivan
Johnny Carson
Mary Tyler Moore
Jerry Seinfeld

Bill Cosby
Barbara Walters
A famous TV personality from your country

POSTREADING

DISCUSSION

1. What are the pros and cons of the fact that TV creates instant celebrities?

2. It has been said that television influences everyone but pleases no one fully. In what ways is this true?

3. Television has the power to bring real-life events into our homes as they are happening. How has this changed our perception of events all over the world? What are the most memorable events you have watched on TV?

4. Robert DeNiro has said, "Being a Hollywood star is death as far as I'm concerned. I don't want people to recognize me in the streets."[1] Dustin Hoffman agrees. He says, "One thing about being successful is that I stopped being afraid of dying. Once you're a star, you're dead already."[2] Would you like to be a celebrity? Do you think it's possible for people like DeNiro, Hoffman, or Oprah Winfrey to lead a normal life?

5. Commenting on her success, Lucille Ball once said, "Love yourself and everything else falls into place." Do you agree or disagree with this statement?

6. Commenting on her achievements and ambition, Oprah Winfrey said, "When I look into the future, it's so bright it burns my eyes." What do you think she means by this?

JUST FOR FUN

WORD PLAY

The word **ENTERTAINMENT** contains thirteen letters. Using only these letters, make as many other words as you can. You may not use the same letter twice unless it appears twice in the word. Do not use proper names or foreign words.

_____   _____   _____

_____   _____   _____

_____   _____   _____

_____   _____   _____

_____   _____   _____

_____   _____   _____

READER'S JOURNAL

Choose a topic that relates to the readings in this unit, and write for about ten to twenty minutes. Consider using one of the quotes or one of the discussion questions in this unit as the basis for your writing.

READER'S JOURNAL

Date: _____

ENTREPRENEURS IN THE ELECTRONIC AGE

Selections

We have seen in recent years how technology can change our lives in the blink of an eye. The latest wave of change is occurring in the way we shop: cybercommerce is taking over. The readings in this unit explore the ways that electronic retailing, with its convenience, personalization, and discounts, is luring customers away from traditional stores and changing the way people do business.

POINTS TO
PONDER

DISCUSSION

Think about and then discuss the following questions.

1. Have you ever ordered anything from a catalog? Have you ever bought anything online?

2. Do you prefer to buy things from a store, where you can actually see and touch the items?

3. Do you think that online shopping will ever replace shopping at stores and malls? Why or why not?

Jeff Bezos is a pioneer on the frontier of Internet commerce. He is the founder and CEO of a successful online bookstore called amazon.com. Bezos knows computers inside and out, but the success of his venture with amazon.com proves that he is also a talented entrepreneur. In the following article, "The Virtual Route to Happiness," Bezos discusses the plan and development of this new retailing concept.

BEFORE YOU READ

PREREADING
ACTIVITY

1. Read the first paragraph of the article. In small groups, make a list of twenty possible products that you might like to sell on the World Wide Web.

   _____   _____   _____   _____

   _____   _____   _____   _____

   _____   _____   _____   _____

   _____   _____   _____   _____

   _____   _____   _____   _____

2. Discuss the advantages and disadvantages of each product, and narrow down your list to two products.

   _____

   _____

3. Analyze the two choices and choose the one you think would be the most successful.

   _____

4. Compare your ideas with those of the other groups.

The Virtual Route to Happiness

Jeff Bezos is a new kind of entrepreneur. He runs "the earth's biggest bookstore," but he works from a cubbyhole and his shops number precisely nil.

BY ANN TRENEMAN

1 A few years ago, Jeff Bezos was a whiz-kid executive on Wall Street when he heard a figure that amazed him: use of the Internet's World Wide Web was growing by 2,300 percent a year. He started to dream a little about this. He made a list of 20 possible products that could be sold on the Web and dreamed a bit more. He narrowed it down to two: music or books. He chose books and stopped dreaming.

2 He quit his job, contacted Moishe's Moving and Storage and said he was heading out West, though he didn't know where. His wife MacKenzie began driving cross-country while he wrote up a business plan on his laptop and pondered their final destination. The hi-tech, high-energy city of Seattle was an obvious choice and he called a lawyer to help him set up. Before long he had rented a house and set to work in his garage to create a virtual bookstore that he named after the world's greatest river. It was 1994. Jeff Bezos was 30 years old and he had no idea what was about to happen next.

3 "We were optimistic when we wrote our business plan for amazon.com but we didn't expect to have as many customers and as much success as we have had," he says with a chuckle. "Anybody who had predicted what has happened would have been committed to an institution immediately! It is rather fun to think that two years ago I would put all the packages in the back of my Chevy Blazer and drive them to the post office myself. Now the post office brings 18-wheel trucks and big 40 ft. containers and parks them at the warehouse to be filled up over one day."

4 He laughs again—a rolling, infectious outburst that ends with a big grin. He does this about once a minute, but really you cannot blame him for being so upbeat. Amazon.com—you always pronounce the dot in-house because Bezos always does—is on a roll. It has 2.5 million titles, calls itself the earth's biggest bookstore and was floated on the New York Stock Exchange last year in a deal valuing it at £187m. There are no profits yet—not unusual

in such a young company—but there is a buzz. In Seattle-speak, its growth has been "awesome" and its customers "cool." Even Bill Gates buys his books at amazon.com.

5   To shop at amazon is still a cult sort of thing, but word travels fast on the Net: nine months ago it had 180,000 customers, now it has 610,000 from around the world. It also has lots of new competition, but so far no one can touch its appeal. When it announced that John Updike was going to write the first paragraph in a summer short story contest, calls came in from around the world. Updike wrote the first 289 words to the whodunit called "Murder Makes The Magazine" on July 29. Every day since, tens of thousands of wannabe co-authors have submitted follow-up paragraphs. Six selectors have worked full-time and flat-out to pick one a day. Updike him-

self communicates with amazon by postcard (he is not even remotely on-line) and it is probable that someone may have to collect this Friday's last installment personally. No one thinks the tale that began with Miss Tasso Polk feeling something nasty in the office elevator is great literature but it has been great publicity and a lot of fun.

6   Fun is a big word for Jeff Bezos. "Well, one of the things you find out pretty quickly in bookselling is that people don't just buy books because they need them. They buy them because shopping for them is fun. Many will spend two hours in an afternoon in a bookstore. I do that! I've done that for all my adult life and even for part of my pre-adult life!" He laughs. "Of course in the on-line world you can't do the same kinds of things that you do in the physical world to make bookstores fun. We cannot have the lattes and the cappuccinos and the soft sofas and the chocolate chip cookies but we can do other things that are completely different. This Updike contest is one of those. We've had hundreds of thousands of entries and it's just *fun*."

7   I ask a question referring to a "normal" bookstore and Bezos pauses. "Well, I call them physical bookstores instead of normal." We are sitting in his physical office on the fourth floor of an older building in downtown Seattle. It is tiny, like all the other hundreds of cubbyholes here, and his desk is made out of an old door. Clearly amazon is not too keen on the trappings of the physical world. "We have the best software and the best people but we don't spend money on things that don't matter much," says a spokeswoman.

8   The place is buzzing with Generation X-ers* who work like

* Generation X-ers   People born in the mid-1970s.

maniacs so they can play like maniacs in the great outdoors that surrounds Seattle. The motto "Work Hard, Play Hard" is tacked up on a wall. The lavatories are mauve and there are crayons and construction paper placed along the corridors in case artistic inspiration strikes. This is amazon's fifth location (not counting the garage) since it went on-line in July 1995 and the number of staff has rocketed from five to 480. Its Web site is full of job openings and the lobby has its share of applicants (and a rather weird assortment of art that the receptionist says came with the building and no one has really bothered to sort out).

9   I suspect Jeff Bezos could not care less about a coordinated decor. He is obsessed with the future, not furnishing. "Today we probably know as much as any other company, maybe even more than any other company, about electronic commerce but I can guarantee you that we only know 2 percent of what we will know 10 years from now. This really is something that is going to change the world. This is the Kitty Hawk stage of electronic commerce."

10   It doesn't seem like that on the Website, though. Customers can post their own reviews of any book as well as read others. They can pull up Oprah Winfrey's favorites, read interviews with authors and blurbs and extracts from books. They can search for books by author, subject, title, keyword, ISBN or publication date. Prices are discounted and books usually arrive within a week. You can ask to be e-mailed when certain books come out or consult the experts about what is the best read in certain subject areas.

11   So what about the future? Bezos lights up at this question: "Right now we have on our Website just the tip of the iceberg but what is going to be a big deal is this notion of redecorating the store for each and every customer who walks in the door. So your version of amazon.com should be completely different from anyone else's. I tell people that instead of having 2.5 million titles, what if we just had one title but it was the title that you wanted. Every time you came it was different and every time it blew you away. Picture a 40,000-sq.-ft. superstore with just one holy shrine in the center with one book on it. You walk into this cavernous space and say, 'My God, that is a great book and that is the one I want.' Now that is a successful selling proposition. It works on-line but not in a physical store."

12   Jeff Bezos's personal shrine is a pretty busy place. "Well, I'm reading *Engines of Creation* which is a book about nano-technology. I just finished a science fiction fantasy classic— perhaps it is a little more fantasy than science fiction—called *Nine Princes in Amber.* I am a real science fiction fan. I spent all my summers when I was growing up in a small Texas town which had a tiny library and about one-fifth of it was dedicated to science fiction . . . I read the entire collection! Let me see, what else? There's another science fiction book called *Wyrm* that is about hackers. Yes, I guess there is a hi-tech bias. Yeah, there is."

13   He laughs, again. "But my favorite book of all time is *Remains of the Day* which for me is the perfect novel." Kazuo Ishiguro should probably expect a call from amazon.com any day now about a new writing contest. As Jeff would say, it's a fun idea.

HOW WELL DID YOU READ?

Circle the letter of the choice that best answers the questions or completes the sentence.

1. According to the article, Bezos decided to start an online commerce company _____ .

   a. after hearing about the projected growth of the World Wide Web
   b. because he had always wanted to sell books
   c. after he got fired from his Wall Street job
   d. because he wanted to move to the West

2. The author describes Bezos as _____ person.

   a. a cautious and pessimistic
   b. a serious and domineering
   c. an innovative and upbeat
   d. a bitter and narrow-minded

3. Bezos is _____ .

   a. sure about what will happen to his business in the future
   b. pleasantly surprised at the success of his business
   c. somewhat disappointed in Amazon.com's sales record
   d. worried about competition from physical bookstores

4. Bezos believes that most people _____ .

   a. prefer to buy books online
   b. would rather shop in physical bookstores
   c. like to read science fiction books
   d. don't only buy books when they need them

5. The number of amazon.com customers is _____ .

   a. increasing rapidly
   b. increasing slowly
   c. decreasing rapidly
   d. decreasing slowly

FYi

In recent years, consumer spending on catalog purchases has averaged $48.3 billion per year.

BUILDING READING SKILLS

MAKING INFERENCES

Put a check mark next to the statements you can infer from information in the article.

_____ ✓ 1. Some physical bookstores have comfortable places for customers to relax, and they also serve coffee and dessert.

N _____ 2. Bezos didn't like his job on Wall Street.

_____ ✓ 3. Expensive furniture isn't a priority for Bezos.

199

_____✓_____ 4. Amazon.com keeps moving to bigger locations as the company continues to grow.

_____N_____ 5. Bezos likes to talk and think about the future.

_____N_____ 6. Science fiction is Jeff Bezos's favorite type of literature.

_____N_____ 7. Most of amazon.com's customers ask to be e-mailed when certain books come out.

_____✓_____ 8. Many of amazon.com's employees are hard-working young people.

_____✓_____ 9. There are advantages and disadvantages of shopping in physical bookstores.

_____N_____ 10. Many companies do not show a profit in the first years of business.

**BUILDING
READING SKILLS**

UNDERSTANDING
REFERENCES

Write the word or phrase that the highlighted reference refers to.

1. *Now the post office brings* 18-wheel trucks and big 40-ft. containers *and parks* **them** *at the warehouse to be filled up over one day.*

   them = _____

2. *We cannot have the lattes and the cappuccinos and the soft sofas and the chocolate chip cookies but we can do* other things that are completely different. *This Updike contest is* **one of those.**

   one of those = _____

3. *We are sitting in* his physical office *on the fourth floor of an older building in down-town Seattle.* **It** *is tiny, like all the other hundreds of cubbyholes here, and his desk is made out of an old door.*

   It = _____

4. *Today we probably know* as much as any other company, *maybe even more than any other company, about* electronic commerce *but I can guarantee you that we only know 2 per cent of what we will know 10 years from now.* **This** *really is something that is going to change the world.*

   This = _____

5. *Right now we have on our Website just the tip of the iceberg but* **what** *is going to be a big deal is this* notion of redecorating the store for each and every customer *who walks in the door.*

   what = _____

EXPANDING VOCABULARY

Using a dictionary, write the part of speech for each word, the meaning as it is used in the article, any synonyms for the word, and a sentence to help you remember the meaning. For the last three items, choose words from the article that were unfamiliar to you.

1. ponder (¶2)

   part of speech: _____

   definition: _____

   synonyms: _____

   sentence: _____

   _____

2. chuckle (¶3)

   part of speech: _____

   definition: _____

   synonyms: _____

   sentence: _____

   _____

3. installment (¶5)

   part of speech: _____

   definition: _____

   synonyms: _____

   sentence: _____

   _____

4. weird (¶8)

   part of speech: _____

   definition: _____

   synonyms: _____

   sentence: _____

   _____

5. version (¶11)

   part of speech: _____

   definition: _____

   synonyms: _____

   sentence: _____

   _____

6. cavernous (¶11)

   part of speech: _____

   definition: _____

   synonyms: _____

   sentence: _____

   _____

7. proposition (¶11)

   part of speech: _____

   definition: _____

   synonyms: _____

   sentence: _____

   _____

8. _____ (¶   )

   part of speech: _____

   definition: _____

   synonyms: _____

   sentence: _____

   _____

9. _____ (¶   )

   part of speech: _____

   definition: _____

   synonyms: _____

   sentence: _____

   _____

10. _____ (¶   )

part of speech: _____

definition: _____

synonyms: _____

sentence: _____

_____

**RESPOND IN
WRITING**

You are about to write a paper about the benefits of online commerce. In one
of the paragraphs, you are going to use amazon.com as an example of a retail
store on the Internet. On a separate piece of paper, make a list of facts from
the article that you could use to support the following point: *There are many
advantages to shopping for books at amazon.com.*

Use your list to write the first draft of the paragraph on separate piece
of paper.

Revise and expand your paragraph, adding information from among the following excerpts from other articles. You may want to refer back to pages
189–190. Use direct quotes or paraphrase the information.

"Explains Bezos, 'Books are a very unusual product category in that there are
so many out there. If you look at music, which is the number two product category, there are about 200,000 active music CDs. If you look at the book category, there are 1.5 million English language books active at any time. If you figure
it worldwide and across all languages, the number is about 3 million. When
you have a huge number of products like that, that's when computers start to
be helpful because of their organizing, sorting, and searching capabilities.'"[2]

"Let's say your friend's birthday is coming up. Amazon will know from its
databank which sorts of books . . . he likes. You then can choose a gift and ship
it off with a few mouse clicks. No drive to the mall. No waiting at the post
office. No rummaging around for a misplaced or out-of-date address."[3]

"Amazon.com has realized 20% to 30% sales increases monthly, which Bezos
credits to unmatched convenience in service, plus access to books that conventional bookstores cannot match."[4]

"Bezos emphasizes that a successful online retailer must add enough value to
convince potential customers to try a new way of shopping—buying habits are
difficult to change."[5]

Read the following passage. The author uses figurative language to describe amazon.com and Jeff Bezos. Underline the words and phrases the author uses figuratively.

What does a bookstore have in common with the world's longest river? The answer is no joke—the online bookseller amazon.com shares more than just a name with the South American river. While the Amazon River spans half a continent, amazon.com the bookstore spans something even larger—the World Wide Web. While other retailers are struggling to attract customers online, CEO and founder Jeff Bezos has charted a high-growth path through the online jungle.

The 33-year-old Bezos is exploring new territory with an old map: adding value and eliminating fears to ease people into a new way of doing business. But instead of aiming for quick profit like the conquistadors of old, Bezos is determined to reinvest revenues for long-term growth—and he's succeeding with an annual growth rate of 3,000 percent. Now the challenge for Bezos is to make amazon.com the winner in the Internet free-for-all as major booksellers like Barnes & Noble and Borders follow the trail he's blazed online.[6]

TALK IT OVER

DISCUSSION

1. Some people believe that the development of the Internet rivals the invention of the printing press. In what ways have both revolutionized the way information is spread?

2. What kind of competition do "physical" bookstores present to online bookstores? In what ways is it preferable to buy in a physical store? In an online store?

The expression *shop till you drop* is often used to describe people who like to shop. Although the title, "Click Till You Drop" does not rhyme, it is a clever way of describing electronic shopping.

BEFORE YOU READ

PREREADING ACTIVITY

Would you rather do the following online or in the real world?

	Online	In the real world
1. buy books	_____	_____
2. buy music CDs	_____	_____
3. book airplane reservations	_____	_____
4. plan a vacation	_____	_____
5. make hotel reservations	_____	_____
6. buy clothes	_____	_____
7. buy groceries	_____	_____
8. buy perfume and cosmetics	_____	_____
9. get information about new cars	_____	_____
10. buy a car	_____	_____
11. get information about computers	_____	_____
12. buy a computer	_____	_____
13. buy and sell stocks	_____	_____
14. get information about real estate	_____	_____
15. buy appliances	_____	_____
16. buy electronic equipment	_____	_____
17. buy personal computer hardware and software	_____	_____
18. enjoy entertainment	_____	_____
19. order flowers	_____	_____
20. buy jewelry	_____	_____
21. buy sports equipment	_____	_____

Click Till You Drop

The Internet has become a shopper's paradise, stocked with everything from wine to cars. Business will never be the same.

By Michael Krantz

1 I know we're not normal," Jerry Yang says with a boyish grin, making a halfhearted effort to straighten up his cubicle for his visitor. It's not much of an office by mogul standards: just a nondescript desk, a couple of cheap plastic milk crates bulging with papers, an old futon. Magazines are piled in a corner, and a window offers a distinctly déclassé view of the parking lot.

2 Of course, by the standards of David Filo, 32, Yahoo's other co-founder, 29-year-old Jerry's digs are West Coast Donald Trump. Filo's office is truly a Goodwill collection truck of a workspace, with dirty socks and T shirts jumbled in with books, software and other debris. Even more startling is his office computer: a poky clone running an outdated Pentium 120 chip. Why wouldn't the chief technologist of the Internet's No. 1 website use the top of the line? Filo just shrugs. "Upgrading is a pain."

3 Could this be the face of 21st century capitalism? You'd better believe it. Two years ago, conventional wisdom still derided the World Wide Web as an amusing toy with little practical application. No more. With striking speed, the business that Yahoo (or, as the company formally calls itself, Yahoo!) has been pioneering has grown into nothing less than a new economic order, a Net Economy! whose exclamation point came last week, when shares of Yahoo surged to more than $200 (closing at $181 on

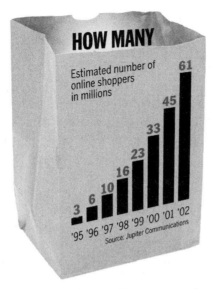

HOW MANY

Estimated number of online shoppers in millions

3 '95
6 '96
10 '97
16 '98
23 '99
33 '00
45 '01
61 '02

Source: Jupiter Communications

Friday), making billionaires of two young men who just a generation ago would only be beginning their climb up the organization ladder.

4   Instead they're already creating a world that is about to become your own. The Net economy that Yang and Filo are building doesn't exist merely in the 115 million Web-page views that Yahoo serves up to hungry surfers every day nor in the stock-market pyrotechnics that have given their venture an explosive $8 billion valuation. The real economy exists in the thousands—even tens of thousands—of sites that together with Yahoo are remaking the face of global commerce. Want to snag a $900 suit for $150? Try *countryroadfashions.com* (but be warned: they're based in Thailand, so you'll have to take your own measurements). Looking for that hard-to-find anthropology book? *Amazon.com* is your best bet. Yearn to have your weekly groceries delivered to your door? *Peapod.com* exists to make your grocery shopping easier—and it even lets you specify how ripe you like your bananas. How about if you want to know the difference between several brands of

stereo receivers? Try *Compare.Net*, which offers a free online buyer's guide that allows users to compare features on more than 10,000 products.

5   And that's the pitch for this new electronic world: faster, cheaper, better. It's the same line we've heard for decades from computer manufacturers, stereomakers and software firms like Microsoft. "Information at your fingertips" is what Bill Gates called it as far back as 1990. Then it was an unimaginably seductive vision. Now it has become a lucrative reality for a select few. *Compare.Net* for instance, has grown from four employees to nearly 40 in less than two years, and its revenue growth is a stunning 25%—every month. Yahoo's lucre spreads beyond Yang and Filo. Just ask the dozens of other post-pubescent millionaires who prowl the firm's Santa Clara, Calif., headquarters. Barefoot.

6   The real promise of all this change is that it will enrich all of us, not just a bunch of kids in Silicon Valley. With online price comparisons, automatic grocery shopping and the ability to get whatever we want whenever we want it, 21st century Americans will face a radical reshaping of the consumer culture we've been building since the 1950s. Think, for a second, about the revolution that shopping malls created in the 1970s and 1980s. They defined not only how we bought stuff but also how we spent our time. The malls themselves became essential parts of a new suburban design, where castles of consumption shaped town layouts in the same way the Colosseum shaped Rome. At its heart, cybercommerce isn't just about building businesses either. It is also, explains Yang, about building a new culture of convenience and speed.

7   It's an attractive idea. According to the GartnerGroup, online consumer sales will reach $20 billion, an increase of 233% over this year's estimated $6.1 billion. And online commerce between companies (places like Boeing that now buy computers online from Dell) is growing even faster. In 1998, says the GartnerGroup, business-to-business trades over the Internet will total $15.6 billion—and by 2000 that figure will reach $175 billion. "The new economy," says Joe Carter, managing partner at Andersen Consulting, "could rapidly overtake the existing economy as we know it."

8   There are skeptics. Stephen Roach, chief global economist at Morgan Stanley Dean Witter, suspects that e-commerce is being oversold, though he admits it's growing rapidly. "I question if it'll ever be big." He is right when he notes that e-commerce is no more than 1% of the U.S.'s $8.5 trillion economy; in fact, consumer online sales now account for only .2% of total retail. And e-commerce, Roach argues, is hardly on a par with the Industrial Revolution. "This is an intangible cerebral revolution, which is a lot harder to pull out."

9   But for hundreds of front-line businesses, this cerebral revolution has become very real. And very unpleasant. Talk to the folks at 230-year-old *Encyclopaedia Britannica*, which two years ago dismissed its entire home sales force in North America after the arrival of the Internet at $8.50 a month made the idea of owning a $1,250, 32-volume set of books seem less appealing. Kids, everyone knew, were just as happy to get their information online or from a CD ROM. In fact, they preferred it. The 170 year-old *Journal of Commerce*, which made most of its money from publishing shipping logs every week, has been forced to set sail on a new digital ocean in order to survive. "The future is electronic," says publisher Willy Morgan, who shed 65 staff members and hurriedly set up a website last year when he discovered advertisers were junking the paper in favor of the Net.

10 They have usurped an old financial term, disintermediation, and given it a new meaning to describe what happened to *Britannica*. To them it means the removal of middlemen, the intermediaries who smooth the operation of any economy—folks like travel agents, stockbrokers, car dealers and traveling salesmen. These people are the grease of a consumer economy, the folks who help you do things more efficiently than you could do them alone. But that's all changing: the Net is creating a new, self-service economy. Gates, who was late in recognizing the value of the Net, nonetheless has come up with the mot juste for this development: he calls it "frictionless capitalism."

11 Say you're planning a trip. Two years ago, you would have phoned your travel agent. But now the complex, proprietary database systems that control the world's airplane-reservations systems are available online and free, reduced to a set of Web pages so simple that even technophobes can book a trip to Paris. And at sites like *priceline.com*, you can actually tell the computer what you're willing to pay for a ticket and then wait to see if it can find an airline that's willing to take you. But will this replace your traditional travel agent? Do you really want to do your own travel planning? That's the crux of the conflict at the heart of this new economy: which services will survive and which will fail,

who will invent new ideas (and reap new millions) and who will close up shop, as useless today as buggy-whip manufacturers became when Henry Ford built the Model-T.

12 Few businesses illustrate this sort of generational corporate conflict better than the book-selling industry. If you want a snapshot of the e-economy, 1998, you could do worse than Jeff Bezos, the founder of bookseller amazon.com. One day last week, as his stock price rose and fell with typical volatility, he stalked through his shuttered Seattle office, on a phone call, staring at his wristwatch, pacing, talking, thinking, plotting, scheming, then glancing at the watch again. Like the Net Economy, Bezos is all about motion.

13 His conversion to the Web came in 1995, when he read a report that projected annual Web growth at 2,300%. First he checked that he'd read the figure correctly. Then he quit his job as a hedge-fund manager in New York City, packed his bags and drove out to Seattle. Or, rather, his wife drove; Bezos was busy pecking out a business plan on his laptop.

14 The idea behind amazon.com was devilishly simple: type in a book's title, the author's name or even just a general subject, and the site will present you with a list of every matching book in its database. Choose your title, type in your address and credit-card number, and service reps at amazon.com's Seattle warehouse will find your order and mail it to you, usually within one or two days, and often at a hefty discount. Three years after launch, amazon.com has 2.25 million worldwide customers, and sales that may reach $350 million this year.

15 None of this, you can imagine, made bookstore chains very happy. But they

Between 1994 and 1998, Internet retail sales jumped from $2.4 to $10 billion. Sales on the Internet are projected to rise to over $1 trillion in the next few years.

held back on the Net. For years the buzz in the book industry was all about building new megastores, where shoppers could sip mochaccinos and chew over big ideas while they sat on comfortable couches. And in the two years that Barnes & Noble and Borders were focusing on what kinds of vanilla-sugar cubes to put in their coffee bars, Bezos was building an empire. B&N has tried to catch up, forging close ties with the gigantic online service America Online and suing amazon.com over its use of the tag line "Earth's Biggest Bookstore."

16 Barnes & Noble has been an object lesson to the rest of the retail world, where everyone seems to have a Net commerce story these days. "In many ways this is what we've been doing for nearly 100 years," says Randy Heiple, vice president of advertising production for catalog giant Spiegel Inc., which ventured online in 1995 and has been ravenously growing ever since. Today the Net accounts for less than 5% of the Spiegel catalog's overall sales, but that share has grown fivefold or more in each of the past three years; sales and circulation of Spiegel's catalogs, meanwhile, have plunged.

17 But even as Spiegel has jumped into the electronic world, other giant retailers have not. Sears, for instance, is taking a more cautious approach. Though it put a catalog of Craftsman tools online last fall, it isn't rushing to build a webstore. "We think it has to be a profitable channel for plans to add any new merchandise for sale," says Paula Davis, a spokesperson for the retailer. But is Sears missing an opportunity? It has already missed Lisa Fontes, a 36-year-old Massachusetts psychologist who went to *sears.com* last month hoping to buy a freezer. The Sears site,

however, didn't have what she needed. "I assumed I couldn't find it because I was stupid or computer illiterate," she explains. But the real illiteracy may have belonged to Sears. It doesn't yet sell freezers online.

18   Sears may feel the chill soon. Most businesses are finding that the Net is actually pretty lucrative. According to ActivMedia, which surveyed 2,000 commerce-related websites, 46% are profitable and an additional 30% expect to cross that line in the next couple of years. For some firms, the Net has become an essential competitive advantage. Dell, which sells $5 million worth of computers a day on its website, claims that the efficiencies of Web-based sales give it a 6% profit advantage over its competitors. Discount-mortgage broker American Finance and Investment, which conducts 60% of its business online, was profitable 90 days after plugging into the Net. And Eddie Bauer, the outdoor-clothing retailer, has an online operation that has been profitable since 1997 and is growing at 300% to 500% a year. The Net, says Judy Neuman, the firm's vice president of interactive media, "makes you think very differently about your customers."

19   And customers have begun to think differently as well. Charles Hintz, a retired psychiatrist from Des Moines, Iowa, has found a kind of salvation in the Net's limitless ease and bounty. Hintz, a 68-year-old quadriplegic, was paralyzed in a fall 12 years ago, but for the past three years he has been doing the birthday and holiday shopping for his large family on the computer, which he operates by poking the keyboard with a stick he holds in his mouth. He buys clothes from Lands' End online, CDs from CDnow and books from amazon.com. "It makes me feel independent," he explains.

20   That, of course, is the real miracle of the Internet. It's not just that it lets you do things better; it lets you do things you couldn't even dream of doing before. The seduction of being online—and this applies to everyone, from novice surfers on AOL to the hardiest hackers on the Web—is that it really does put an awful lot of power in your hands. You can start with the simplest of questions—How do I buy a new sport-utility vehicle?—and step away from your PC in an hour with more information than you might have gathered in a month without a modem. And that information may be better than anything you've ever seen. *Carpoint.com*, the Microsoft website, lets you look at 3D, interactive pictures of the inside of dozens of sports cars—something you can't do anywhere in the real world. The virtual world, for all its hype and promise, is finally delivering on at least one big idea: information, at last, is at your fingertips. This is what explains—even justifies—Jerry and David's billions. More fingertips start their Web travels at *Yahoo.com* than at any other site.

WHAT

Estimated online revenues by industry in millions (1998)

Travel	$2,091
PC hardware	$1,816
Groceries	$270
Gifts/flowers	$219
Books	$216
PC software	$173
Tickets	$127
Music	$81
Clothing	$71

Source: Jupiter Communications

21   For Yang and Filo, it's been a strange ride. Filo, a shy, laconic man who radiates intense smarts, remembers when he could visit every site on the World Wide Web in a couple of hours. That was in early '94, when the Web was young, and Jerry, his more outgoing partner, used to record the best web-sites on his computer for fun. The two shared offices in a trailer at Stanford University that was big enough for a desk and computer for each of the graduate students.

22   David developed a navigational guide to search the Web, and soon Jerry found himself keeping track of not only his favorite sites but also David's. They dubbed their growing list "Jerry's Guide to the World Wide Web." But their part-time hobby quickly grew into a full-time obsession. More and more of their friends wanted to keep up with what was happening on the Web, and by fall the two enthusiasts were surfing the Net day and night. "It was impossible even to sleep," says Yang. Clearly there was a demand for some sort of service that could organize and make sense of all that information out there in cyberspace. They decided to turn their sideline into a business.

23   Their first meeting with a venture capitalist, Michael Moritz of Sequoia Capital, was all they needed. "With no promotion, no advertising and just word of mouth, something was happening," Moritz recalls. "Jerry and David had developed something for themselves that, I think probably to their great surprise and consternation, was as attractive to other people as it was to them." Moritz took a gamble on the entrepreneurs and gave them $1 million for a 25% stake (it turned out to be a good bet—that stake would

WHERE

Top shopping sites (May 1998)

	Business
bluemountainarts.com	Cards
amazon.com	Books
cnet.com	Software
columbiahouse.com	Music
ebay.com	Auctions
cdnow.com	Music
barnesandnoble.com	Books
hotfiles.com	Software
netmarket.com	Market
musicblvd.com	Music

Source: Media Metrix

now be worth around $2 billion). Stanford told them they could keep the venture on campus at least initially, which they did. And they called themselves Yahoo. . .

24   In the spring of 1995, Yang and Filo put their doctoral theses on hold and moved into their first office, in nearby Mountain View, in the heart of Silicon Valley, near some railroad tracks. It was a relatively big suite, around 1,700 sq. ft., which they needed for the computer servers that would gather and store the data, and the people who would feed and care for them. But by the end of the year they needed more space and moved into a 12,000-sq.-ft. site in Sunnyvale, where they went public. "We thought, 'This is great. We'll never fill this place up,'" recalls Yang. Wrong. Last year, after moving into a 33,000-sq. ft. floor of a Santa Clara industrial park, they spread onto two additional floors in a neighboring building for a total of nearly 100,000 sq. ft.

25   The lure of megasites like Yahoo is that in a place like the Net—where people tend to go wherever they want with ease—here are very few

locations that attract a mass audience of the sort that advertisers can get through, say, the Superbowl. As a result, search and commerce sites like Yahoo and chief rival Excite have become gateways (the Net buzz word is portals) to the rest of the electronic universe. And owning a portal is looking a lot like owning a toll bridge. Yahoo charges about 4¢ for every ad it serves up on many of its 115 million pages every day. And those prices will rise as Yahoo develops technology that lets it more closely match advertisers with searchers.

26   That notion—of personalized content and advertising—has been a kind of Internet holy grail for years. Now, finally, the Web is delivering. Its tens of thousands of sites can match your needs and desires as quickly as your Pentium can get online. It's possible to get everything from custom newspapers to electronic newsletters that alert you to sales of items you've always craved. Futurists used to call these services "The Daily Me," a play on the idea of daily newspapers. But customized websites are delivering something more like "the instant me"—real-time collections of just the information you want, which you can use to shop, buy a stock or plan a last-minute trip. In our 20th century consumer culture, it may seem almost too good to be true: the latest and greatest products, custom-made and delivered whenever you want! And how to pay for all this online bounty? We hope you've bought some Yahoo stock.

● ●

HOW WELL DID YOU READ?

A. Read the following statements. If a statement is true, write *T* on the line. If it is false, write *F*.

_____ 1. Consumer sales on the Internet have been steadily increasing.

_____ 2. The new Net economy will probably benefit only a few young entrepreneurs.

_____ 3. Shopping malls created a revolution in the 1970s and 1980s.

_____ 4. The Net economy has hurt some front-line retail businesses.

_____ 5. Sears is taking a cautious approach to the world of electronic commerce.

_____ 6. Jerry Yang and David Filo were initially surprised at their success.

B. Answer the following questions in complete sentences.

1. Why are some people skeptical about the importance of e-commerce?

   _____

   _____

2. How did shopping malls create a revolution in the 1970s and 1980s?

   _____

   _____

3. How have front-line businesses been hurt by the Net economy?

   _____

   _____

4. In what ways is the Net creating a new self-service economy?

   _____

   _____

EXPANDING VOCABULARY

Using a dictionary, write the part of speech for each word, the meaning as it is used in the article, any synonyms for the word, and a sentence to help you remember the meaning. For the last two items, choose words from the article that were unfamiliar to you.

1. startling (¶2)

   part of speech: _____

   definition: _____

   synonyms: _____

   sentence: _____

   _____

2. lucrative (¶5)

   part of speech: _____

   definition: _____

   synonyms: _____

   sentence: _____

   _____

3. radical (¶6)

part of speech: _____

definition: _____

synonyms: _____

sentence: _____

_____

4. intangible (¶8)

part of speech: _____

definition: _____

synonyms: _____

sentence: _____

_____

5. ravenously (¶16)

part of speech: _____

definition: _____

synonyms: _____

sentence: _____

_____

Total U.S. retail sales were $2.5 trillion in 1998.

6. plunge (¶16)

part of speech: _____

definition: _____

synonyms: _____

sentence: _____

_____

7. laconic (¶21)

part of speech: _____

definition: _____

synonyms: _____

sentence: _____

_____

8. consternation (¶23)

   part of speech: _____

   definition: _____

   synonyms: _____

   sentence: _____

   _____

9. _____ (¶   )

   part of speech: _____

   definition: _____

   synonyms: _____

   sentence: _____

   _____

10. _____ (¶   )

   part of speech: _____

   definition: _____

   synonyms: _____

   sentence: _____

   _____

BUILDING READING SKILLS

EXAMINING MEANING

Read each of the following sentences from the article carefully. Then, circle the letter of the sentence that is closest in meaning to the original.

1. *Two years ago, conventional wisdom still derided the World Wide Web as an amusing toy with little practical application.*

   a. Two years ago the opinion about the World Wide Web was that it was both amusing and practical.
   b. Two years ago the prevailing opinion scorned the World Wide Web, saying it was just an impractical toy.
   c. Two years ago most people thought the World Wide Web was neither amusing nor practical.

2. *The real promise of all this change is that it will enrich all of us, not just a bunch of kids in Silicon Valley.*

   a. All this change promises to enrich everyone except a bunch of kids in Silicon Valley.
   b. All of us promise that the change will enrich a bunch of kids in Silicon Valley.
   c. All of this change promises to enrich not only a bunch of Silicon Valley kids, but all of us.

3. *According to ActivMedia, which surveyed 2,000 commerce-related websites, 46% are profitable and an additional 30% expect to cross that line in the next couple of years.*

   a. ActivMedia surveyed 2,000 commerce-related Websites and found that 46% are profitable now and 30% more expect to be profitable soon.
   b. According to a survey by ActivMedia, 46% of commerce-related Websites are already profitable, but 30% of them will not be in the next few years.
   c. ActivMedia expects that while 30% of commerce-related Websites are profitable, 46% will soon be.

4. *With striking speed, the business that Yahoo (or, as the company formally calls itself, Yahoo!) has been pioneering has grown into nothing less than a new economic order . . .*

   a. With amazing speed Yahoo's business has become nothing.
   b. The business that Yahoo has been pioneering has become less than a new economic order.
   c. The business that Yahoo has been pioneering has become a new economic order very quickly.

5. *It's not just that [the Internet] lets you do things better; it lets you do things you couldn't even dream of doing before.*

   a. In addition to letting you do things better, the Internet lets you do things you couldn't imagine doing in the past.
   b. The Internet doesn't let you do things better, but it does let you do things you couldn't even dream of doing in the past.
   c. The Internet lets you do things better, but not things you couldn't do before.

BUILDING READING AND WRITING SKILLS

INTERPRETING CHARTS AND GRAPHS

1. Complete the paragraph with information from the chart.

In a recent profile of online shoppers in the United States, the median age was found to be _____ . Of those who buy online, _____ are professionals, _____ have a college degree, and _____ have children under age eighteen who live at home. The average household income of online shoppers is _____ . On the whole, _____ people are more likely to shop online than _____ people.

WHO

Profile of online shoppers in the U.S.

Median age _____ 33
Average household income _____ $59,000
Single _____ 59%
Married _____ 41%
Children under 18 at home _____ 34%
College degree _____ 57%
Professional _____ 30%

Source: Jupiter Communications

2. Finish this paragraph using information from the chart.

WHY NOT

Reasons for not buying online

Fear of hackers _____ 21%
Lack of products _____ 16%
Can't see the products _____ 15%
Must reveal personal information _____ 13%
Poorly designed site _____ 8%
Companies' reputation _____ 6%
Afraid of money or merchandise getting lost _____ 6%

Source: World Research

There are several reasons that people do not buy online. The highest percentage, 21%, cited _____ as the most important reason. _____

_____

_____

_____

_____

_____

_____

_____

_____

_____

217

3. On a separate piece of paper, write a paragraph based on information in the chart.

BUILDING READING SKILLS

INCREASING
READING SPEED

You will have 20 seconds in which to underline the word that is the same as the first word in each line.

1. share	hair	hare	shape	shore	share
2. left	theft	leave	leg	left	felt
3. hurt	hurt	hung	runt	rang	truck
4. mark	marker	marked	marks	mark	mart
5. nice	spice	nice	neat	knick	nine
6. speak	speaker	speaks	peak	speak	spoke
7. news	new	none	nine	newsy	news
8. group	grope	grand	group	grown	gown
9. cry	cringe	rye	crime	cry	cried
10. book	book	boon	boom	brook	boot
11. after	after	alter	attend	agent	again
12. pour	pours	poured	pouch	pound	pour
13. had	hack	hand	had	has	half
14. white	while	whiff	wind	white	win
15. luck	lull	lucid	lucky	lug	luck

When you have finished, figure out how many answers you got right and check the appropriate box on page 263 in order to keep track of your progress.

Corporations are not the only settings for cybercommerce. Read the following article to learn how the practice of medicine is also coming online.

ACROSS CYBERSPACE

CYBERMEDICINE SEEN AS UNHEALTHY BY SOME

By Aaron Zitner

Patients come from all over the world for treatment by Dr. Steven Kohler, an emergency room physician at Salem Hospital. It is a very speedy trip. All they have to do is log on and tell the doctor where it hurts—by electronic mail.

From their office on the Internet, Kohler and fellow Salem Hospital physician Kerry Archer have been diagnosing ailments and prescribing medication for two years to people around the globe. Now, a host of doctors are rushing online, prompting questions about whether Internet medicine is good medicine.

"When we started, a lot of doctors said this is heresy," Kohler said. "But as time goes on, doctors and more of the public will see this as a significant aspect of the practice of medicine."

Kohler calls it the "virtual housecall." A woman on vacation contracts a urinary tract infection, and she needs an antibiotic. A man on a business trip has a relapse of asthma, and he wants an inhaler. Kohler says these are typical, minor ailments that can be evaluated in the live, person-to-person electronic exchanges offered for $50 by his Internet site, called CyberDocs (www.cyberdocs.com).

The potential for "cybermedicine" could be huge. It is a low-cost way to match doctors with patients, 24 hours a day, whether the patient lives in remotest Alaska or crowded Somerville.

At the Physician Insurers Association of America, which represents malpractice insurers, an official says she has received at least a dozen inquiries from doctors in the last six months about setting up sites like Cyberdocs. Relatively low overhead costs make it an attractive business prospect: Kohler says he and Archer have spent about $80,000 on their site and that it has begun to break even. They claim 20 to 30 consultations weekly, with about 90 percent involving a request for prescription drugs.

But cybermedicine also raises a thicket of red flags. Can doctors really treat patients they have never seen? Will patients try to obtain drugs they do not need? Will doctors practice in areas where they have no expertise?[7]

BUILDING WRITING SKILLS

SUMMARIZING

Write a one-paragraph summary of the main ideas of the article above.

_____

_____

_____

_____

_____

_____

_____

_____

READ AND REACT

UNDERSTANDING VISUAL POETRY

For centuries, poets have known that part of our enjoyment in reading a poem comes from the way it looks when we see it in print. Many poets have experimented with the appearance of their poems, understanding that form affects the reader's appreciation. Poetry is traditionally thought of as writing that appears in short lines and expresses both emotions and experiences. Visual poetry, however, conveys the poet's meaning through an arrangement of letters, words, or symbols.

A. Answer the questions.

1. Look at the following poem. What shape does the poet want us to see?

2. What are the separate words the poet intends us to read?

<pre>
          acom
         puterm
        ouseisju
        stlikean
        yotherm
         ousea
           l
          wa
              ysind
                ange
                   rofa   ttack
                     CATa
</pre>

3. What does the shape of the poem have to do with the words?

4. What does the poet want to indicate by capitalizing the word *cat*?

5. What does a cat represent in this poem?

6. Does the author use any figurative language in the poem?

7. What is the tone of this poem? What is the poet's attitude toward computers?

8. Look at a computer mouse. What liberty did the poet take in designing the visual poem?

9. Examples of visual poetry can be found in many different languages. Are you familiar with any such poems in your native language? What is your opinion of visual poetry?

B. Work together in small groups of two or three to create a visual poem.

1. Begin by choosing a familiar object such as a tree, sun, hand, house, or heart.

2. Write down words or phrases you can think of that relate to that object.

3. Decide on and then draw the outline of the object you want to use.

4. Fill in the outline as appropriate.

5. Make a final copy of your visual poem.

6. Compare your poem with that of other groups.

POSTREADING

DISCUSSION

Read and discuss the following questions.

1. What types of products do you think are best suited for sale over the Internet?

2. What are the advantages and disadvantages of shopping online?

3. What do you think about the issues that the practice of cybermedicine raises? Can doctors really treat patients they have never seen? Do you think patients will try to obtain medicine they don't really need? How can be cybermedicine be monitored? Do you think doctors should have a special license to practice online?

4. The nineteenth-century writer Edward Bellamy said, "Buying and selling is essentially anti-social." In contrast, the nineteenth-century philosopher John Stuart Mill believed that "Trade is a social act." Which one do you agree with?

JUST FOR FUN

WORD SEARCH

The business- and technology-related words on the next page were used in the articles in this unit. Find them in the word search puzzle. The words may be horizontal, vertical, or diagonal. One word has been found for you. Then check your answers in the Answer Key on page 264.

virtual	electronic	click
superstore	commerce	retail
bookstore	software	surfing
technology	firms	megasites
Internet	website	consumers
amazon	online	keyboard
entrepreneur	shopping malls	hackers
book	database	cubbyhole

```
A X T F R O S M W R Z E L E C T R O N I C P O R R C
N E(V I R T U A L)R E T Z M F S U V I L U W F U I X
X Z F O T I P U Z R Y X N B K G M P C K B L O Z U L
P X E A R R E O O P K M Q L S R I R O J B P M K D S
O Q T P C A R T D J M E G A S I T E S F Y B O O K L
T I O E T X S O R T Z F J T O N U Q Z L H N G A E T
R K E T I K T R C A B R B T I T E C H N O L O G Y A
V S A O O F O U Q M O N L I N E Q R E X L T I O B U
B L I O R O R S T P F J G L O R E N T E E L B A O R
T P B R E A E P B F N Z S E T N L O M L X Y U R A Z
V E R A P H U Z I N T C P S N E M E P R E M T O R I
N J H F N I Z Q U J L A I E R T R E D I D Z A O D T
S H O P P I N G M A L L S F I I R I W F I R M S O E
L F I T Q P W N Z B I A O M N W R E I N Z Q I U Z M
F N A R K P R A N T B I F L E O Q N P I N R T B Y O
C W A S B L O R B A O R T E C O M M E R C E O T J Z
R E T A I L Z A T R M O W F L A C S H F E Z T I U T
B B F N Q J G A R Z P M A E I Q R F I Z Y N L F B L
R S A B D C D M L Y O Z R Y C E N B T O J U E O I L
A I F X I O N A V R C E E D K E L R L E G E B U S M
K T R B U A B Z E E S O L C D E O C O N S U M E R S
H E I Z L O R O D R T G A N E R P Y A L I A I N H R
Y A S U R F I N G M N H T C V J U R Z E Y C N P A Z
E N F T O I L K Y D R A O F Z A P O J E L T M W H I
```

READER'S JOURNAL

Choose a topic that relates to the readings in this unit, and write for about ten to twenty minutes. Consider using one of the quotes or one of the discussion questions in this unit as the basis for your writing.

READER'S JOURNAL

Date: _____

IQ OR EQ ?

FYi

Unit·8

Selections

For many years intelligence has been measured by IQ tests. New research, however, indicates that there is more to intelligence than what shows up on IQ tests. As you work through the readings in this unit, you will explore some of the character traits that seem to be as critical as intellect in determining success in life.

Think about and then discuss the following questions.

1. How do you think success in life should be measured? What qualities do you think successful people share?

2. Generally speaking, are you controlled more by your head or your heart?

3. How good are your interpersonal skills?

SELECTION I

BEFORE YOU READ

PREREADING
DISCUSSION

At some point in our lives most of us wish that we could be as smart as Einstein, as multi-talented as da Vinci, as gifted as Mozart. For years researchers have tried to figure out the characteristics that make someone a genius. In "The Art of Genius," we learn that creativity is a key factor and that creativity is not the same as intelligence.

1. How would you define the word *genius*?

2. Do you know anyone who is a genius?

3. When you think of the word *genius*, what comes to mind? On a separate piece of paper, freewrite for ten minutes on the topic of *genius*. Write as much as you can as fast as you can without worrying about mistakes.

The Art of Genius

Eight ways to think like Einstein

By Michael Michalko

1   How do geniuses come up with ideas? What links the thinking style that produced *Mona Lisa* with the one that spawned the theory of relativity? What can we learn from the thinking strategies of the Galileos, Edisons, and Mozarts of history?

2   For years, scholars tried to study genius by analyzing statistics. In 1904, Havelock Ellis noted that most geniuses were fathered by men older than 30, had mothers younger than 25, and usually were sickly children. Other researchers reported that many were celibate (Descartes), fatherless (Dickens), or motherless (Darwin). In the end, the data illuminated nothing.

3   Academics also tried to measure the links between intelligence and genius. But they found that run-of-the-mill physicists had IQs much higher than Nobel Prize-winner and extraordinary genius Richard Feynman, whose IQ was a merely respectable 122. Genius is not about scoring 1600 on your SATs, mastering 14 languages at the age of 7, or even being especially smart. As psychologist Joy P. Guilford and others have demonstrated, creativity is not the same as intelligence.

4   Most people of average intelligence can figure out the expected conventional response to a given problem. For example, when asked "What

is one-half of 13?" most of us immediately answer six and one-half. That's because we tend to think *reproductively*. When confronted with a problem, we sift through what we've been taught and what has worked for us in the past, select the most promising approach, and work within a clearly defined direction toward the solution.

5   Geniuses, on the other hand, think *productively*. They ask "How many different ways can I look at this problem?" and "How many ways can I solve it?" A productive thinker, for example, would find a number of ways to "halve 13":

6.5

1 3 = 1 and 3

THIR TEEN = 4

XI II = 11 and 2

XIII = 8

The mark of genius is the willingness to explore *all* the alternatives, not just the most likely solution. Asked to describe the difference between himself and an average person, Albert Einstein explained that the average person faced with the problem of finding a needle in a haystack would stop when he or she located a needle. But Einstein would tear through the entire haystack looking for all possible needles.

6   Reproductive thinking fosters rigidity. This is why we so often fail when we're confronted with a new problem that appears on the surface to be similar to others we've solved, but is, in fact, significantly different in its deep structure. Interpreting such a problem through the prism of past experience will inevitably lead you astray. If you think the way you've always thought, you'll get what you've always gotten.

7   For centuries the Swiss dominated the watch industry. But in 1968, when a U.S. inventor unveiled a battery-powered watch with no bearings or mainspring at the World Watch Congress, every Swiss watch manufacturer rejected it because it didn't fit their limited paradigm. Meanwhile, Seiko, a Japanese electronics company, took one look at the invention and proceeded to change the future of the world watch market.

8   Biologists have long known that a gene pool lacking in variation will sooner or later be unable to adapt to changing circumstances. In time, the genetically encoded wisdom will convert to foolishness, with consequences fatal to the species. Similarly, we all have a rich repertoire of ideas and concepts based on past experiences that enable us to survive and prosper. But without any provision for variation, they become stagnant and ineffectual.

9   When Charles Darwin returned to England after his famous trip to the Galapagos Islands, he showed the finch specimens he found there to distinguished zoologist John Gould. But Gould didn't know how to interpret them. Thinking the way he had been conditioned to think, he assumed that, since God made one set of birds when he created the world, the specimens from different locations would be identical. As a result, he thought Darwin's finches, which looked quite different from the English variety, represented a distinct species—and missed the textbook case of evolution right in front of him. As it turned out, Darwin didn't even know the birds were finches, but because of his unorthodox way of thinking, he came up with an idea that would reshape the way we see the world.

10   By studying the notebooks, correspondence, and conversations of some of the world's great thinkers in science, art, and industry, scholars have identified eight thinking strategies that enable geniuses to generate original ideas.

11 *1* ***Geniuses*** *look at problems from all angles.*

Einstein's theory of relativity is, in essence, a description of the interaction between different perspectives. Sigmund Freud's analytical methods were designed to find details that didn't fit traditional paradigms in order to come up with a completely new point of view. To solve a problem creatively, you must abandon the first approach that comes to mind, which usually stems from past experience, and reconceptualize the problem. Thus geniuses do not merely solve existing problems; they identify new ones.

12 *2* ***Geniuses*** *make their thought visible.*

Once geniuses have a certain minimal verbal facility, they develop visual and spatial abilities that allow them to display information in new ways. The explosion of creativity in the Renaissance was intimately tied to the development of graphic illustration during that period, notably the scientific diagrams of Leonardo da Vinci and Galileo Galilei. Galileo revolutionized science by making his thought graphically visible while his contemporaries used more conventional means. Similarly, Einstein thought in terms of spatial forms, rather than along purely mathematical or verbal lines. In fact, he believed that words and numbers, as they are written or spoken, did not play a significant role in his thinking process.

13 *3* ***Geniuses*** *produce.*

Thomas Edison held 1,093 patents, still the record. He guaranteed a high level of productivity by giving himself idea quotas: one minor invention every 10 days and a major invention every six months. Johann Sebastian Bach wrote a cantata every week, even when he was sick or exhausted. Wolfgang Mozart produced more than 600 pieces of music. In a study of 2,036 scientists, Dean Keith Simonton of the University of California at Davis found that the most respected scientists produced more "bad" works than their less successful peers.

14 *4* ***Geniuses*** *make novel combinations.*

Like playful children with buckets of building blocks, geniuses constantly combine and recombine ideas, images, and thoughts. Einstein didn't invent the concepts of energy, mass, or speed of light; he simply combined them in a novel way. The laws of heredity were developed by Gregor Mendel, who combined mathematics and biology to create a new science of genetics.

15 *5* ***Geniuses*** *force relationships.*

Their facility to connect the unconnected enables geniuses to see things others miss. Da Vinci noticed the similarity between the sound or a bell and a stone hitting water—and concluded that sound travels in waves. Organic chemist F. A. Kekule intuited the shape of the ringlike benzene molecule by dreaming of a snake biting its tail. When Samuel Morse was trying to figure out how to produce a telegraphic signal strong enough to transmit coast to coast, he observed teams of horses being exchanged at a relay station. His solution? Give the traveling signal periodic boosts of power.

16 *6* ***Geniuses*** *think in opposites.*

Geniuses, according to physicist David Bohm, are able to think differently because they can tolerate ambivalence between two incompatible subjects. Another physicist, Niels Bohr, argued that if you hold opposites together in your mind, you will suspend your normal thinking process and allow an intelligence beyond rational thought to create a new form. Example: Bohr's ability to imagine light as both a particle and a wave led to his conception of the principle of complementarity.

17 **7 Geniuses** *think metaphorically.*

Aristotle believed that the ability to perceive resemblances between two separate areas of existence—to think metaphorically, in other words—is a special gift. Alexander Graham Bell compared the inner workings of the ear to a stout piece of membrane moving steel—and, in the process, conceptualized the telephone. Einstein made some of his most stunning discoveries by drawing analogies between abstract principles and everyday occurrences such as rowing a boat or standing on a platform watching a train pass by.

18 **8 Geniuses** *prepare themselves for chance.*

Whenever we attempt to do something and fail, we end up doing something else. That's the first principle of creative accident. We may ask ourselves why we have failed to do what we intended, which is a reasonable question. But the creative accident leads to the question: What have we done? Answering that one in a novel, unexpected way is the essential creative act. It is not luck, but creative insight of the highest order.

19 Alexander Fleming was not the first physician studying deadly bacteria to notice that mold formed on an exposed culture. A less gifted physician would have dismissed this seemingly irrelevant event, but Fleming thought it was "interesting" and wondered if it had potential. It did: penicillin. One day, when Edison was pondering how to make a carbon filament, he found himself mindlessly twisting a piece of putty in his fingers. He looked down at his hands and found the answer to his problem: Twist the carbon like rope.

20 This may be the most important lesson of all: When you find something interesting, drop everything and go with it. Too many talented people fail to make significant leaps of imagination because they've become fixated on their preconceived plan. But not the truly great minds. They don't wait for gifts of chance; they make them happen.

● ●

HOW WELL DID YOU READ?

Read the following statements. If a statement is true, write *T* on the line. If it is false, write *F*.

_F_ 1. The statistical data about geniuses compiled by researchers like Havelock Ellis were very enlightening.

_T_ 2. Creativity is not the same as intelligence.

_F_ 3. Most people tend to think productively, whereas geniuses tend to think reproductively.

_T_ 4. According to the author, the mark of genius is the willingness to explore the alternatives, not just the most likely solution.

_____F___ 5. The Swiss watch industry was quick to accept the idea of a battery-powered watch.

_____I___ 6. Darwin's unorthodox way of thinking led to an idea that changed the way we look at the world.

BUILDING READING SKILLS

MAKING INFERENCES

Put a check mark next to the statements that you can infer from information in the article.

_____✓___ 1. Productive thinking is more flexible than reproductive thinking.

_____✓___ 2. Having an extremely high IQ is not always a prerequisite for genius.

_____✓___ 3. Biologists believe that a gene pool must have variation to be able to adapt to changing circumstances.

_____✓___ 4. Seiko was thinking productively when it embraced the idea of a battery-powered watch.

_____✗___ 5. Analyzing statistics is the best way to study genius.

_____✓___ 6. Geniuses aren't fixated on a preconceived plan and are therefore able to make leaps of imagination.

BUILDING WRITING SKILLS

PARAPHRASING

According to the article, scholars have identified eight thinking strategies that enable geniuses to generate original ideas. In your own words, explain each of the eight strategies.

1. _Geniuses look at problems from all angles._

_____

_____

_____

2. _Geniuses make their thought visible._

_____

_____

_____

3. *Geniuses produce.*

_____

_____

_____

4. *Geniuses make novel combinations.*

_____

_____

_____

5. *Geniuses force relationships.*

_____

_____

_____

6. *Geniuses think in opposites.*

_____

_____

_____

7. *Geniuses think metaphorically.*

_____

_____

_____

8. *Geniuses prepare themselves for chance.*

_____

_____

_____

BUILDING READING SKILLS

IDENTIFYING EXAMPLES

Scan the article to identify which strategy each of the following examples represents. Write the number of the strategy (1–8) on the line provided.

1. Gregor Mendel combined mathematics and biology to create the science of genetics.   Strategy: _____4_____

2. Sigmund Freud's analytical methods found details that didn't fit into traditional models to come up with a new point of view.   Strategy: ____1____

3. Niels Bohr's ability to imagine light as both wave and particle led to the principle of complementarity.   Strategy: ____6____

4. Alexander Fleming noticed mold forming on bacteria and discovered penicillin.   Strategy: ____8____

5. Galileo Galilei revolutionized science by making his thoughts graphically visible.   Strategy: ____2____

6. Leonardo da Vinci noticed the similarity between the sound of a bell and a stone hitting water and concluded that sound traveled in waves. Strategy: ____5____

7. Wolfgang Mozart produced more than 600 pieces of music. Strategy: ____3____

8. Alexander Graham Bell conceptualized the telephone by comparing the inner workings of the ear to a stout piece of membrane moving steel. Strategy: ____7____

EXPANDING VOCABULARY

Using a dictionary, write the part of speech for each word, the meaning as it is used in the article, any synonyms for the word, and a sentence to help you remember the meaning. For the last item, choose a word from the article that was unfamiliar to you.

1. inevitably (¶6)

   part of speech: _____

   definition: _____

   synonyms: _____

   sentence: _____

   _____

2. paradigm (¶7)

   part of speech: _____

   definition: _____

   synonyms: _____

   sentence: _____

   _____

3. stagnant (¶8)

part of speech: _____

definition: _____

synonyms: _____

sentence: _____

_____

4. distinguished (¶9)

part of speech: _____

definition: _____

synonyms: _____

sentence: _____

_____

5. abandon (¶11)

part of speech: _____

definition: _____

synonyms: _____

sentence: _____

_____

6. contemporaries (¶12)

part of speech: _____

definition: _____

synonyms: _____

sentence: _____

_____

7. novel (¶14)

part of speech: _____

definition: _____

synonyms: _____

sentence: _____

_____

8. ambivalence (¶16)

   part of speech: _____

   definition: _____

   synonyms: _____

   sentence: _____

   _____

9. analogy (¶17)

   part of speech: _____

   definition: _____

   synonyms: _____

   sentence: _____

   _____

10. _____ (¶   )

   part of speech: _____

   definition: _____

   synonyms: _____

   sentence: _____

   _____

RESPOND IN WRITING

On a separate piece of paper, write a paragraph describing your thoughts about one of the following quotes.

1. "There was never a genius without a tincture of insanity." (Aristotle[1])

2. "Creativity is more than just being different. Anybody can play weird—that's easy. What's hard is to be as simple as Bach. Making the simple complicated is commonplace—making the complicated simple, awesomely simple—that's creativity." (Charles Mingus[2])

3. "Everybody is born with genius, but most people only keep it a few minutes." (Edgard Varese[3])

A *prodigy* is a child with exceptional talent or ability. Mozart is one of the best-known examples of a child prodigy. Read the following short articles about prodigies in chess, music, and math.[4]

THEY BURN SO BRIGHT

Prodigies are the last acceptable freak show. We gawk at them, wondering how long their creative fires will stay alive.

Jorge Zamora

Maybe Jorge's grades at Oliver Hazard Perry Middle School in Providence, R.I., were low this past year because he read chess magazines in class. He's the best chess player in the United States under 16, and he comes by the title almost genetically. His father and brother are both masters, and by the time Jorge was 7, he was too good to play against other kids. "Chess is like falling in love for me," he says—but it's not a smooth romance. In 1990 his family moved from Honduras to the United States so he could complete at a higher level. Now they may move to New Jersey so Jorge can be closer to tournaments in New York. Yet at the same time, says Jorge, "my dad gets mad and says I'm smart. I should get A's. I think he's right. When I study for 15 minutes, the next day I do get A's." It's clear that Jorge is torn. At 14 he wants to be like everyone else so the kids won't laugh at him—and he wants to stand out as a champion. But he sees the pressures of that life. "To be an engineer of computers or a doctor, you don't have to be the best to make a living," he says. "But to make a living playing chess you have to be really at the top."

Sarah Chang

There is no more precarious—or engaging—prodigy than the musician, for she puts her talent on public display. While dazzling technique may carry a youthful career, it cannot alone support an adult one. But Sarah Chang, a 12-year-old violinist from Philadelphia, already performs with an adult's emotional grasp. Dorothy DeLay, the celebrated Juilliard teacher, is well acquainted with prodigy; her pupils include Itzhak Perlman and Midori. She first heard Chang when she was 5 and took her on soon after. DeLay was amazed at her technical proficiency but truly astonished by "her attempt to make a musical phrase. I'd never seen anything like it." Chang, the daughter of Korean-born musicians, has a recording contract with EMI (her latest disc is a passionate reading of the Tchaikovsky concerto) but limits her concert dates. And even the whiz-kid fiddler doesn't really get to cut class: on the road, she faxes in her homework.

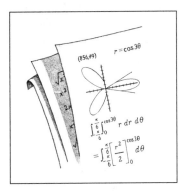

Lenny Ng

Imagine—and it takes some doing—Lenhard (Lenny) Ng, the older son of Cantonese immigrants who settled in Chapel Hill, N.C., where his father is a physics professor at the University of North Carolina. At 10, he scored a perfect 800 on the math SAT. He set a record by performing flawlessly, four years running in the American High School Math Exam. Last year he won a gold medal at the math olympics in Moscow. He took honors in several violin and piano competitions and played on a championship little-league basketball team while earning all A's at UNC (he attended high school and college simultaneously). Julian Stanley, who founded the Study of Mathematically Precocious Youth at Johns Hopkins University, calls him "the most brilliant math prodigy I've ever met." This fall Ng will enter Harvard, probably as a sophomore. He is 16. It's enough to make you hate him—except that he is a genuinely nice kid. "I have a lot of friends." says Ng. "I've tried to live as normal a life as possible. People say to me, 'You're a math god' And I say, 'I am?'" And this will make you feel better: on his verbal SAT last year, Ng got a mere 780.

ORAL REPORT

Research one of the following prodigies. Look for information about his or her childhood, significant achievements, and influence on society. Prepare a five-minute oral presentation for your class.

Isaac Manuel Francisco Albéniz

Jeremy Bentham

John Stuart Mill

Wolfgang Amadeus Mozart

Eugene Ormandy

Blaise Pascal

Alexander Pope

Pierre Auguste Renoir

Juana Inéz de la Cruz

Itzhak Perlman

Midori

a famous prodigy from your country

TALK IT OVER

DISCUSSION

1. It seems that there are fewer true geniuses today than there were fifty years ago. According to psychologist Dean Keith Simonton, one explanation might be the extreme specialization of science today. "A narrow specialist has less chance of making the novel combinations that add up to genius than does a scientist knowledgeable about several disciplines."[5] Do you agree or disagree with this explanation?

2. Psychologist and author Howard Gardner "thinks that . . . creative geniuses tend to 'return to the conceptual world of childhood,' and are able to 'wed the most advanced understandings' of a field 'with the kinds of problems, questions, issues and sensibilities that most characterize . . . a wonder-filled child.'"[6] What qualities of a child do you think geniuses emulate?

DILBERT reprinted by permission of United Feature Syndicate, Inc.

BEFORE YOU READ

PREREADING
DISCUSSION

The following article is entitled "The E-Factor!" The "E" stands for "enthusi-asm." Psychologists have long focused on negative emotions such as depression and anxiety, but they are now seriously studying positive qualities such as enthusiasm. As you read the article, think about your own temperament and your outlook on life.

1. Generally speaking, are you an optimist or a pessimist?

2. How would you define the word *enthusiastic*?

3. Do you think of yourself as an enthusiastic person? Why or why not?

BUILDING READING SKILLS

PREVIEWING

Before you read the article, spend a few minutes previewing it by completing the following steps.

1. Read the title and subtitle. Think about what it means, and try to predict what the general topic of the article might be.

2. Read the headings that are written in bold print. How do you think the author will develop the topic? Try to anticipate the kind of information that might be included in each section of the article.

3. Read the first and last paragraphs. What technique does the author use to introduce the topic in the first paragraph? What conclusion does she make in the last paragraph?

4. Read the first sentence of each paragraph, and think about how the article is organized and how the topic is developed.

5. Make a list of points you think the author might discuss in the article.

_____

_____

_____

_____

_____

_____

The E-Factor!

Good news! We can all develop the quality that can
make you happy, successful—even thin.

By Mary C. Hickey

1   When I first met my friend Carol, I was convinced she was the luckiest woman alive. It seems like everything in her world is always wonderful. She describes her husband as "the greatest guy you could meet" and her job in real-estate sales as "loads of fun." When she talks about places she's been or people she's met, she uses words like *awesome, fabulous* and *terrific*.

2   But over the years as I've gotten to know her better, I've realized that, really, Carol is no luckier than anyone else. Like all of us, she has her share of ups and downs. What is special about her, though, is her attitude: No matter what happens, Carol looks at the bright side. She somehow manages to remain upbeat, energetic, vivacious. She is absolutely and totally . . .

3   Enthusiastic!

4   For a time, the cynical side of me found Carol's incessantly cheerful spirit a bit much. (I mean, really, how can anyone be happy all the time?) But more and more, I've grown to admire—even envy—this character trait. I've seen how Carol's enthusiasm works for her. She does well at her job, has lots of friends and always seems to enjoy what she's doing.

5   What's more, I'm increasingly finding Carol delightful to be around. Her upbeat spirit is contagious, even for skeptics like me. Whenever I'm with her, I can actually feel my own enthusiasm bubble to the surface. And, the fact is, that sure beats feeling cynical.

THE WINNING EDGE

6   What's behind this E-factor, that magical quality called enthusiasm? Why do some people have it in abundance? And, most important, what can those of us who don't come by it naturally do to develop it?

7   Unfortunately, there are no hard-and-fast answers to these questions. Though researchers have long focused on negative emotions like depression and anxiety, it's only recently that psychologists have begun serious study of enthusiasm.

8   Already, though, scientists know enough to confirm what Norman Vincent Peale intuitively sensed back in 1952 when he first published his now-classic book, *The Power of Positive Thinking*. That is, that the character traits of enthusiastic people are typically associated with greater peace of mind, higher self-esteem, a stronger sense of well-being and even better physical health and increased success in school and in the workplace.

9   "People who have a positive mental outlook have a distinct edge in life over others who are less enthusiastic," says psychiatrist Harold Bloomfield, M.D., co-author of *The Power of 5* (Rodale Books, 1995) and numerous

other top-selling self-help books that teach, among other things, how to become more enthusiastic.

10   Indeed, the benefits of a positive outlook are wide ranging. C.R. Snyder, Ph.D., a professor of psychology at the University of Kansas, in Lawrence, found that students who had positive expectations about their school performance actually performed better than those who didn't. In a study of college freshmen, Snyder and his colleagues discovered that the level of expectation among these students at the beginning of the semester was a better predictor of their grades than their high-school grade-point averages. And research on women on diets shows that those who maintained a positive outlook about their success were quicker to lose weight.

11   In fact, new research suggests that qualities like optimism and enthusiasm may actually somehow trigger our own immune systems into work-

ing more effectively. A study of college students at the University of Michigan, for instance, found that pessimistic students were ill twice as many days as optimistic students and had four times as many doctor's visits over the course of a year.

AN AMERICAN TRADITION

12   Yet for all its positive values, enthusiasm isn't exactly in fashion these days. In fact, in a world characterized by chaos and confusion, the prevailing mood seems to be one of suspicion and cynicism. A recent Roper poll found that Americans' level of optimism about the future has been steadily declining since the late eighties: Only a fifth of the people surveyed today feel the American Dream is very much alive, compared to a third of those who felt that way in 1986.

13   But social observers say this may be a fleeting malaise; the reality is that an upbeat spirit is deeply embedded into the American character. "There has always been a strain of positive optimism and enthusiasm in this country," notes Charles Bassett, Ph.D., professor of English and American Studies at Colby College, in Waterville, Maine.

14   Adds Frank Farley, Ph.D., a psychologist at Temple University, in Philadelphia, "A spirit of enthusiasm persists in our culture today."

THE ROOTS OF ENTHUSIASM

15   What exactly is enthusiasm? Where does the trait come from? Why do some people, like my friend Carol, seem to be brimming with so much of the E-factor, while other people (myself included) can get enthusiastic about one thing and remain matter-of-fact about something else?

16   Experts believe a number of things are involved. Some say it's learned

behavior that is either encouraged or quashed during childhood.

17 But genetics may also play a role. "Some people seem to be born with a lot of joy juice," says Auke Tellegen, Ph.D., a professor of psychology at the University of Minnesota, in Minneapolis, who has been researching a personality trait he calls "positive emotionality," a clinical term that is synonymous with enthusiasm.

18 According to Tellegen, research suggests that a person's level of positive emotionality may be related to heightened levels of a brain chemical called dopamine, though it is not clear exactly what causes this chemical to be produced in abundance. But some studies suggest that enthusiasm may also be an inherited trait. Tellegen cites research involving identical twins who, though raised in different families, typically share the same level of enthusiasm.

MY QUEST FOR ENTHUSIASM

19 But what happens if you haven't inherited the E-gene? Is it possible to raise your level of enthusiasm and live life a little more fully?

20 Inspired by my friend Carol, I recently decided to find out. Not that I'd been particularly unhappy or anything, but my fortieth birthday was on the horizon, and I felt that it was time to start enjoying life more. So about six months ago, I made a conscious effort to try to be more enthusiastic about things, and remarkably, it seems to be working.

21 How did I do it? I went to the library and borrowed an armload of self-help books and tapes by motivational speakers, and at a card store, I found some posters and refrigerator magnets with such sentiments as "Attitude: It's a Small Word That Makes a Big Difference!" "When Life Hands You a Lemon, Make Lemonade!" and "Don't Sweat the Small Stuff. And Remember, It's All Small Stuff!"

22 Frankly, not all of it was for me (the more I listened to a tape on enthusiasm by one motivational speaker, for instance, the sillier it sounded). But at the same time, I did manage to find lots of good stuff.

23 I've become conscious of my tendency to think of excuses for why I can't do something instead of concentrating on why I can. For example, when a friend asked me to try in-line skating, I put aside my initial reaction (*Are you kidding? I'll break my legs*) and forced myself to reconsider (*If I can ice-skate, I'm sure I can do this, too*). I've been rolling along ever since—enthusiastically.

24 I've started giving myself little pep talks whenever I find myself falling into a slump. On the bus on my way home from work, for example—a time when I'd normally agonize over my difficulties juggling a job, a house and a family—I close my eyes and tell myself how lucky I am. I've got a *fabulous* home! An *awesome* job! A *wonderful* husband! And two of the most *terrific* kids in the world. (*Honest, they are!*)

25 No, I'll never be a bubbly spirit like my friend Carol. I don't even aspire to bubblyhood. It's just not my style. And part of being enthusiastically upbeat, I've come to realize, is accepting yourself for who you are. But that doesn't mean it isn't possible to make some minor adjustments. The fact is that I *have* added a little more joy juice to my life—and if I can do it, anyone can. Now *that's* something to get really enthusiastic about!

HOW WELL DID YOU READ?

Circle the letter of the choice that best completes the sentence or answers the question.

1. Which sentence best expresses the main point of the article?

    a. Students who have a positive attitude perform better in school.
    b. Enthusiasm is basically an inherited trait that is difficult to alter.
    c. Developing a more enthusiastic attitude can make you more successful and happier.
    d. Enthusiasm is something you cannot acquire.

2. The author's feelings about Carol have _____ .

    a. changed over time
    b. remained the same
    c. become more negative
    d. faded over the years

3. In general, the author's tone is _____ .

    a. formal
    b. conversational
    c. anxious
    d. threatening

4. The author describes her friend Carol as being _____ .

    a. cynical
    b. skeptical
    c. enthusiastic
    d. critical

5. Which statement would the author agree with?

    a. We live in a chaotic and confusing world where most people are cynical and suspicious.
    b. The world today is basically safe and predictable, and people are generally trusting and secure.
    c. Most people are envious of others because our world is so competitive.
    d. Because our world is characterized by chaos and confusion, most people are becoming increasingly optimistic.

6. According to a recent survey, the number of people who feel the American Dream is still very much alive _____ .

    a. is increasing
    b. has remained the same
    c. is decreasing
    d. is unpredictable

243

7. The author believes that _____ .

   a. it is impossible to become a more enthusiastic person
   b. there is no reason to change your level of enthusiasm
   c. it is possible to train yourself to become more enthusiastic
   d. motivational tapes are the best way to become more enthusiastic

8. According to the article, which of the following are involved in a person's level of enthusiasm?

   a. genetics
   b. learned behavior in childhood
   c. heightened levels of dopamine
   d. all of the above

9. The article mentions research that has been done on all of the following except _____ .

   a. the relationship between optimism and enthusiasm and the workings of our immune system
   b. the effect of a positive outlook on women who are dieting
   c. the effects of enthusiasm on job performance
   d. the correlation between positive outlook and performance in school

10. Research involving identical twins who were raised apart but shared the same level of enthusiasm was cited to support the idea that _____ .

   a. twins are generally more enthusiastic than singletons
   b. identical twins who are raised apart tend to be less enthusiastic than those raised together.
   c. identical twins share a level of enthusiasm similar to that of the general population
   d. enthusiasm may be an inherited trait

EXPANDING VOCABULARY

Using a dictionary, write the part of speech for each word, the meaning as it is used in the article, any synonyms for the word, and a sentence to help you remember the meaning. For the last item, choose a word from the article that was unfamiliar to you.

1. vivacious (¶2)

   part of speech: _____

   definition: _____

   synonyms: _____

   sentence: _____

   _____

2. cynical (¶4)

   part of speech: _____

   definition: _____

   synonyms: _____

   sentence: _____

   _____

3. incessantly (¶4)

   part of speech: _____

   definition: _____

   synonyms: _____

   sentence: _____

   _____

4. abundance (¶6)

   part of speech: _____

   definition: _____

   synonyms: _____

   sentence: _____

   _____

5. confirm (¶8)

   part of speech: _____

   definition: _____

   synonyms: _____

   sentence: _____

   _____

6. prevailing (¶12)

   part of speech: _____

   definition: _____

   synonyms: _____

   sentence: _____

   _____

7. suspicion (¶12)

   part of speech: _____

   definition: _____

   synonyms: _____

   sentence: _____

   _____

8. sentiments (¶20)

   part of speech: _____

   definition: _____

   synonyms: _____

   sentence: _____

   _____

9. agonize (¶23)

   part of speech: _____

   definition: _____

   synonyms: _____

   sentence: _____

   _____

10. _____ (¶   )

   part of speech: _____

   definition: _____

   synonyms: _____

   sentence: _____

   _____

RESPOND IN WRITING

Choose one of the following expressions from the article, and write on a separate piece of paper about an experience from your life that either proves or disproves its validity.

"Attitude: It's a small word that makes a big difference!"

"When life hands you a lemon, make lemonade."

"Don't sweat the small stuff. And remember, it's all small stuff."

**BUILDING
READING SKILLS**

INCREASING
READING SPEED

You will have 20 seconds in which to underline the word that is the same as the first word in each line.

1. except	accept	exchange	except	excuse	exact
2. lash	latch	lavish	leash	lash	laser
3. odd	off	of	ode	odd	odds
4. some	some	somber	soon	soot	song
5. refine	refined	refill	refund	reform	refine
6. true	trust	trunk	true	truth	truck
7. sail	sale	salt	said	lace	sail
8. under	undo	over	under	undone	undue
9. ant	art	tan	ate	ant	rat
10. cost	coast	cost	costs	costly	can
11. fire	first	fish	fill	fine	fire
12. jazz	jaws	zap	jazzy	jazz	jeans
13. work	wake	work	rake	cake	wore
14. hand	hung	hunk	hunt	hand	hind
15. assist	assistant	asset	assign	assert	assist

When you have finished, figure out how many answers you got right and check the appropriate box on page 263 in order to keep track of your progress.

Daniel Goleman holds a Ph.D. in psychology from Harvard and is a science writer for the *New York Times.* In his best-selling book, *Emotional Intelligence,* he describes the results of behavioral research into how the human mind processes feelings. His premise is that emotional skills are at least as important as IQ in determining an individual's success in life. By "emotional skills" he means the ability to identify and regulate feelings, empathize with others, control impulses, and deal with setbacks. In an interview in "The Lowdown on High EQ," Goleman explains his theory.

1. In what ways do you think it is possible that emotional well-being and temperament can be more helpful to success in life than standard intelligence?

2. Who do you think has better interpersonal skills: men or women? Why?

3. Do you think men or women deal better with stress?

The Lowdown on High EQ

By Timothy Dumas

1   Forget IQ as a measure of smart, says the author of a current runaway best-seller. The true predictor of success resides in our emotions!

2   Americans have been dumb about intelligence for a long time. But in *Emotional Intelligence,* the surprise best-selling book of the season, Daniel Goleman jolts awake educators, business leaders, and common folk, too, by attempting nothing less than to redefine what it means to be smart.

3   Our traditional focus on cognitive intelligence—the stuff measured by IQ tests—explains little about the reasons we succeed in our work and relationships and the reasons we fail. Why does the kid with the highest IQ in the class wind up in a humdrum job? Why do bright people engage in

chronic stupidity—from making bad money decisions to hurting those they love? The answers lie in failures not of IQ but of EQ—emotional intelligence.

4   Goleman cites five basic elements of high EQ: awareness of your feelings as you experience them; empathy, or awareness of what others are feeling; managing your moods; staying motivated and optimistic despite setbacks; and interacting well with other people. If all this sounds suspiciously like what we used to call character, that's essentially what Goleman is talking about. So what's the big news? It's that our increasingly violent and anxious society is suffering an EQ drain, and we're doing far too little to plug it up. We don't even have a clear idea how to.

5   This is where Goleman steps in, bearing good tidings: Although IQ is more or less fixed, we need not settle for static EQ. "All these skills that make up emotional intelligence—every one of them—are learned throughout life," says Goleman, who writes on behavior science for *The New York Times* and has taught at Harvard. "The basic learning is laid down in childhood, but because of the way the brain shapes itself—which is through experience—learning is lifelong and you can improve any of these skills at any point."

6   Listen in as Goleman further elaborates on his theory in response to questions from Cosmo. . . .

7   **Q.** Has our preoccupation with IQ been harmful in that it neglects EQ?

8   **A.** Oh, sure. IQ has been completely oversold. There's been this mystique about people's IQ, as though it were a magical number. Well, for one thing, it's a fallacious number. IQ tests actually are summative of a range of individual skills, like spatial reasoning or verbal fluency. And everyone has an uneven profile. It's more important to know your profile than the average of all those scores. You lose information with an IQ score. It's a very rough and, frankly, relatively meaningless way to rank people. It's more important to know whether a person is verbally fluent if you're considering him for a writing job, say. Is he good at spatial reasoning? Then he might be a good architect. This is a much more meaningful way to look at cognitive intelligence.

9   But what all that has ignored is the critical role in life of this other range of skills—emotional intelligence. It turns out that IQ predicts only about 20 percent of life success, and success is narrowly defined as job success. Which leads to another question: Is job success alone the same as having a successful life? I would say it's not. I know many people with wonderful jobs who lead bleak lives.

10   **Q.** So EQ is a better indicator of our destinies than IQ?

11   **A.** It depends which domain of life you're talking about. If you're talking about how well you'd do as a mathematician, no, it's not. For that, you need the kind of numeric abilities and so on that IQ measures. But very little in life is confined to the narrow domain of cognitive abilities measured by IQ. Most things we do in life call on emotional intelligence. Management, for one, is an emotional-intelligence skill. Sales depend on emotional intelligence. Having a happy marriage or relationship depends on emotional intelligence. Being a good parent, being a good citizen, a caring person in the community—all of that really depends on emotional intelligence, and IQ is largely irrelevant.

¹² **Q.** In your book, you cite a massive study that shows the present generation of children to be more troubled emotionally than the last. What are the implications?

¹³ **A.** The data comes from a national random sampling of kids that was conducted first in the mid-seventies and then in the late eighties; the kids were rated by their parents and teachers. According to the findings, American children, on average, got progressively more deficient in emotional intelligence over the period of a decade and a half. They were more angry, more hot-tempered, more volatile, more anxious, more depressed, more lonely, more sulky, more disobedient, had poorer impulse control—there was a universal deterioration. What's more, violence, depression, and eating disorders among young people seem to be climbing. So the outlook for children isn't very good these days.

¹⁴ **Q.** Does all this mean we as a nation are suffering a breakdown of emotional intelligence?

¹⁵ **A.** I think it's very clear that we are. Scary headlines all bespeak this. Every time we read about another senseless murder, it's a sign of emotional intelligence gone awry. Homicides among young people are up by a factor of four in the last twenty years. Suicides have tripled among young people during the same period. Forcible rape has doubled. These are indicators of what's going on in society, of our collective emotional life.

¹⁶ **Q.** How did our emotional lives start coming apart?

¹⁷ **A.** I think what's happened is that parents and relatives and extended family and neighbors and the whole community aren't there for kids the way they used to be, because of larger social forces. It's not that anyone loves kids less these days. It's just that economic forces mean parents have to work more than they did, so they're unable to spend the kind of time with their children that their own parents spent with them. Family life has changed. There's a saying that it takes a village to raise a child. Villages don't work as well as they used to, and they don't work as well now for kids. More parents live in neighborhoods where they're afraid to have their kids play on the street. God forbid they should go into a neighbor's house! That's a real change of the last twenty, thirty, forty years. Another thing that's happened is more kids are spending more hours glued to a TV set or a computer, which simply means they're not out playing with other kids. You learn emotional intelligence through your interaction with people, and there's less of that going on now.

¹⁸ **Q.** Education is a controversial subject these days, but the debate seems to have little to do with things like emotional intelligence. Should it?

¹⁹ **A.** Absolutely. That's why I wrote the book! The bottom line is that since these emotional qualities are crucial to life, since they're learned to the greatest extent in childhood, since kids aren't learning them anymore, we've got to teach them in school. If I'd had the opportunity to send my kids to a school that taught emotional literacy, I'd have done it in a moment.

²⁰ **Q.** Critics charge that teaching emotional skills in school implies there are "right" emotions, which in turn implies setting up an emotional-values system. What do you think?

²¹ **A.** I don't think it's a very well-informed critique, frankly, because if you look at what they're teaching in emotional-literacy classes, as I have, it's not values; it's not giving kids

moral conundrums to deal with or a new virtue to master. That's something else entirely. About five years ago, a consortium of experts did a survey of all these school-based prevention programs—the war on teen pregnancy, the war on dropping out, the war on drug abuse, the war on violence—and they found out a lot of them didn't work; indeed, some made matters even worse. But some of them did work, and they worked because they taught this core of emotional social skills that kids could build on for life. You teach a kid how to handle his impulses, you teach him how to know what he's feeling, you teach him how to manage anger, you teach him empathy, and you get a better kid.

22 Q. What happens when kids don't learn these lessons?

23 A. Young boys who are impulsive—the kids who always get into trouble in their early elementary school years—they have three to six times greater likelihood of committing violent crimes by the end of their teens. Girls who are impulsive and disobedient in grade school don't get violent; they get pregnant at three times the rate of other girls. So the programs teach kids the basic skills for life, and they're the human skills we've always imparted to our children—things like empathy and caring, expressing your emotions appropriately. I don't see anything wrong with that. There's a lot right with it.

24 Q. Are you saying that low EQ and crime are linked?

25 A. Yes, to a large extent. Crime is linked to a lot of things—most of all poverty. In terms of predicting who among the impoverished are most likely to end up following a criminal path, you have to look at emotional intelligence as a very strong predictor.

It's the kids who are impulsive, the kids who aren't empathic, who go down that path. Empathy is critical in susceptibility to violence. If you're empathic, it's very hard to do harm to another person.

26 My brother-in-law, Leonard Wolf, is a writer—his specialty is horror. Lovely man, though. He was interviewing a serial killer whom he was thinking of writing a book with, and at one point, he said to this really scary guy who had killed ten people and who was known as the Santa Cruz Strangler, "How could you have done that? Didn't you feel any pity for your victims?" And the strangler said, very matter-of-factly, "Oh, no, if I'd felt any of their pain, I couldn't have done it." And it's true. Empathy puts the brakes on acts of violence.

27 Q. Let's talk about the sexes. Are women more emotionally intelligent than men?

28 A. In some ways, yes; in some ways, no. Women, on average, are more empathic than men. That's a key ability. They're better at picking up subtle, unspoken emotional dimensions to interactions. Girls are groomed in the emotions in a way boys aren't, and women are kind of natural emotional managers in a relationship or in marriage. Men have a lot to learn from women about empathy.

29 On the other hand, women aren't necessarily better than men at managing their moods. It's well established that women are twice as likely as men to become depressed, and one reason is the difference between what women do and what men do when they're feeling depression. I'm not talking about extreme, clinical depression but just feeling down. Women tend to like to get together with a girlfriend and talk over what's getting them down. The problem is that ruminating about what's upset you tends to prolong the depressed feeling. So unless your friend is extremely skilled, you may end up being depressed for longer than if you hadn't had the conversation.

30   Men, on the other hand, when they're feeling down, go out and distract themselves. They go to a ball game, a movie, a bar—and it turns out that's a better way to handle depression. Unfortunately, men have double the rate of alcoholism, so it may even out.

31   **Q.** If men and women react differently to emotional distress, what advice do you have for them when they clash?

32   **A.** It's not bad to clash; it's bad if you don't have the right way of working out the disagreement. There are certain patterns of being poor at handling emotions in a marriage that predict a divorce very strongly. One of them is expressing your complaint as a personal attack. Instead of saying, "Dear, it really bothers me when you leave your dirty socks on the floor, because I feel you don't respect me and I have to pick up after you," you say, "You're the biggest slob I've ever seen." And you say it in a tirade. That's inept. It leads to defensiveness, which closes off communication, which might lead you to feel you're not being heard. So you might up the volume and expand the personal attack, and then add some contempt and disgust, which is a very damaging message from someone you love.

33   **Q.** You also write about the workplace. Has the business world, which stands to gain so much by being emotionally intelligent, picked up on your message?

34   **A.** I've had a huge response from the business world. The implications for the workplace are many and great. Just to name one: A lot of people in the business world are promoted because of their technical expertise; they're very good at some cognitive side of the job. But the problem is the Peter Principle—you get promoted to your level of incompetence. So there are a lot of managers and bosses who end up being inept at handling people, even though most of the job now requires management skills rather than technical skills. They're not good at delivering criticism, they blow up at people, they do all kinds of things that emotionally undermine the working climate and make their staffs less effective. That's a real problem throughout the business world.

35   **Q.** What about the maxim that IQ gets you hired but EQ gets you promoted? Do you think that's true?

36   **A.** I think it ought to be. Most personnel people structure their criteria for hiring biased toward technical IQ scores, so the first bar you have to jump over to get into the workplace is, What are your academic credentials? But once you're in the workplace, they should matter less and less. It's the other skills—the ability to express the unspoken feelings in a group, say—that make you a natural leader, for which you should be recognized and then promoted.

37   **Q.** Does professional failure often revolve around some emotional failing?

38   **A.** Almost always! Something about a person's emotional life is sabotaging her or him. Time and again, you see people of great promise in their school performance, test performance, and so on, dead-end in their work life. And usually it's because they can't keep themselves motivated—they give up too easily—or their feelings get in the way of thinking clearly, because they can't handle their moods well or they're inept with other people.

252

have to people-skills

39 Q. You write that academic intelligence and emotional intelligence really have little to do with each other. Is there no correlation at all between the two?

40 A. There's little or none. I was just talking to a man who'd gone to MIT who contended, based on his memories of the student body there, that at the highest end of IQ there's actually a negative correlation. I don't know if that's true, but there's no relationship. You can have high IQ and high EQ—which, of course, is a winning combination—or be high in one and low in the other.

41 The best study was done at Bell Labs in New Jersey, a very high-IQ place. They do research and development for the communications industry. In a division of electronics engineers who were designing equipment so advanced that they worked in teams of up to 150, coworkers and managers were asked to nominate the standouts, the stars in productivity and effectiveness. They came up with ten or fifteen names, and that group of stars was compared with everyone else. It turned out there was no difference in IQ, no difference in academic credentials, no difference in years on the job. What there was a difference in was emotional intelligence.

42 The stars were people who knew how to get along, who knew how to motivate themselves—usually the kind of people you like to hang out with, the kind you trust. When these people ran up against a technical problem that they'd have to turn to someone else for an answer to, they'd E-mail and get an answer right away, because they'd built up networks of people before they needed them. The other people would E-mail and wait up to two weeks for an answer. So you can see how being good in the interpersonal realm actually was a direct benefit even for effectively pursuing a technical task.

43 Q. Who in public life impresses you as being emotionally intelligent?

44 A. Every great leader—from Winston Churchill to Gandhi to Martin Luther King, Jr.—has had to have emotional intelligence. What made them so persuasive was that they could take the emotional pulse of a group and articulate its unspoken shared feelings, and that's a very powerful thing to be able to do as a leader. It makes you a leader. And it allows you to point the way to what needs to be done. But beware of the people who are good at leading and persuading, yet lack empathy. Those are the dangerous leaders who adopt agendas that are heartless.

45 Q. Your book has drawn wide attention out there, touching on both the most public and the most private aspects of our lives. Have you hit on something people are looking for?

46 A. Well, yes. I think people sense that things in our collective emotional life are out of control and that in our personal lives we need a little guidance. I point to the fact that you can improve EQ skills at any age. It's a very hopeful message, and I think people are looking for hope in these dark days.

HOW WELL DID YOU READ?

Reread the first five paragraphs of the article and answer the questions that follow.

1. According to the article, what is the true predictor of our success?

   _____

2. What are the five basic elements of Goleman's definition of a high EQ?

   a. _____

   b. _____

   c. _____

   d. _____

   e. _____

BUILDING READING SKILLS

UNDERSTANDING POINT OF VIEW

Which of the following statements do you think the author would agree with? Put a check mark next to those statements.

_____ 1. Cognitive intelligence explains why we succeed or fail at our work and relationships.

_____ 2. It is easier to improve your EQ than your IQ.

_____ 3. IQ is not a very accurate way to rank people.

_____ 4. Job success is a very good indicator of success in life.

_____ 5. Children today are more emotionally troubled than they were in the past.

_____ 6. Schools should include the teaching of emotional skills in their curricula.

_____ 7. There doesn't seem to be a correlation between the lack of emotional intelligence and crime.

_____ 8. Women are generally more attuned to people's feelings than men are.

_____ 9. The more empathetic you are, the easier it is to do harm to someone else.

_____ 10. Academic intelligence and emotional intelligence are strongly related.

_____ 11. Emotional skills, such as empathy, can be shaped by experience.

BUILDING WRITING SKILLS

SUMMARIZING

In your own words, summarize how Goleman answers each of the following questions.

1. Is EQ a better predictor of our destinies than IQ?

(10)

_____

_____

_____

2. What are the implications of the observation that the present generation of children seems to be more troubled emotionally than the last?

(12)
·
(14)

_____

_____

_____

3. How did our emotional lives start coming apart?

(16)
·
(18, 20)

And how is education part of the solution?

_____

_____

_____

4. What is the relationship between crime and low EQ?

(22 --> (24)

_____

_____

_____

5. How are women's and men's emotional intelligences different?

(27)
·
(31)

What is some good advice for men and women when they clash emotionally.

_____

_____

6. How is the maxim, "IQ gets you hired, but EQ gets you promoted," true?

(33) ->
(35)

_____

_____

_____

7. How does professional failure often revolve around some emotional failing? (37)

_____

_____

8. Is there any correlation between EQ & IQ? (39)

EXPANDING VOCABULARY

Using a dictionary, write the part of speech for each word, the meaning as it is used in the article, any synonyms for the word, and a sentence to help you remember the meaning. For the last item, choose a word from the article that was unfamiliar to you.

1. empathy (¶4)

   part of speech: _____

   definition: _____

   synonyms: _____

   sentence: _____

   _____

2. static (¶5)

   part of speech: _____

   definition: _____

   synonyms: _____

   sentence: _____

   _____

3. elaborate (¶6)

   part of speech: _____

   definition: _____

   synonyms: _____

   sentence: _____

   _____

4. fallacious (¶8)

   part of speech: _____

   definition: _____

synonyms: _____

sentence: _____

_____

5. implications (¶12)

part of speech: _____

definition: _____

synonyms: _____

sentence: _____

_____

6. random (¶13)

part of speech: _____

definition: _____

synonyms: _____

sentence: _____

_____

7. deficient (¶13)

part of speech: _____

definition: _____

synonyms: _____

sentence: _____

_____

8. controversial (¶18)

part of speech: _____

definition: _____

synonyms: _____

sentence: _____

_____

9. impulsive (¶25)

part of speech: _____

definition: _____

synonyms: _____

sentence: _____

_____

10. prolong (¶29)

part of speech: _____

definition: _____

synonyms: _____

sentence: _____

_____

11. _____ (¶   )

part of speech: _____

definition: _____

synonyms: _____

sentence: _____

_____

RESPOND IN WRITING

Reread Goleman's answer to the question, "Who in public life impresses you as being emotionally intelligent?" Choose a political leader from your country, and write a paragraph about his or her emotional skills. Explain how those skills helped make him or her a good leader.

_____

_____

_____

_____

_____

_____

_____

_____

Is this a positive or a negative review of *Emotional Intelligence*? On a separate piece of paper, make a list of the phrases in the review that support your opinion.

EMOTIONAL INTELLIGENCE

By Patricia Hassler

If your class valedictorian did not become the soaring success everyone predicted, perhaps his IQ exceeded his EQ. Psychologist Daniel Goleman's latest book is a fascinating depiction of the role emotional intelligence plays in defining character and determining destiny. He has produced an eminently readable and persuasive work that shows us how to develop our emotional intelligence in ways that can improve our relationships, our parenting, our classrooms, and our workplaces. Goleman assures us that our temperaments may be determined by neurochemistry, but they can be altered. We could turn society on its ear if we learned to recognize our emotions and control our reactions; if we combined our thinking with our feeling; if we learned to follow our flow of feelings in our search for creativity. This well-researched work persuades us to teach our children an important lesson: humanity lies in our feelings, not our facts. This is an engrossing, captivating work that should be read by anyone who wants to improve self, family, or world.[7]

TALK IT OVER

DISCUSSION

1. "When David Campbell and others at the Center for Creative Leadership studied 'derailed executives,' the rising stars who flamed out, the researchers found that these executives failed most often because of 'an interpersonal flaw' rather than a technical inability."[8] Describe a situation you know of in which someone became "derailed" because of an "interpersonal flaw."

2. According to interviews with top executives in the United States and Europe, some of the emotional failings that cause failure in business include "poor working relationships, being authoritarian, being too ambitious, and having conflict with upper management."[9] What other "emotional failings" can you think of that could cause problems in the work environment?

Read and discuss the following questions.

1. How do you think Daniel Goleman would respond to the statement, "The sign of an intelligent person is the ability to control emotion by the application of reason?" (Marya Mannes[10])

2. Albert Einstein once said, "As a human being, one has been endowed with just enough intelligence to be able to see clearly how utterly inadequate that intelligence is when confronted with what exists."[11] Do you agree or disagree with this statement? Give some examples to support your opinion.

3. Respond to this quote: "Intellect is to emotion as our clothes are to our bodies; we could not very well have civilized life without clothes, but we would be in a poor way if we had only clothes without bodies." (Alfred North Whitehead[12])

JUST FOR FUN

WORD SCRAMBLE

Unscramble the letters below to discover words used in this unit. Write each word in the space provided. Then check your answers in the Answer Key on page XX.

1. n i l a c y c

2. v i t y r e a t i c

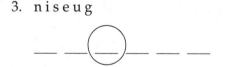

3. n i s e u g

4. g i n e c l i n t e l e

5. m e t h i n u s a s

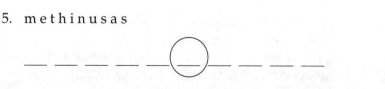

6. t a l i o n e m o

— — — — — —◯— — —

7. t r o c a f

— — —◯— — —

8. r y t e h o

— —◯— — — —

You will notice that eight of the letters are circled. Write the circled letters in the spaces below. Then unscramble them to find the name of someone mentioned in this unit.

— — — — — — — —

9. _____

READER'S JOURNAL

Choose a topic that relates to the readings in this unit, and write for about ten to twenty minutes. Consider using one of the quotes or one of the discussion questions in this unit as the basis for your writing.

READER'S JOURNAL

Date: _____

BUILDING READING SKILLS

INCREASING READING SPEED

Correct Words	Unit 1	Unit 2	Unit 3	Unit 4	Unit 5	Unit 6	Unit 7	Unit 8
15								
14								
13								
12								
11								
10								
9								
8								
7								
6								
5								
4								
3								
2								
1								
0								

UNIT 1   JUST FOR FUN   page 32

REBUS

1. downtown 2. stepmother 3. Count Dracula 4. safety in numbers 5. in the middle of nowhere
6. undershirt 7. side by side 8. coffee break

UNIT 2   JUST FOR FUN   pages 64–65

BRAIN TEASERS

1. twelve 2. short 3. in a chess game 4. There are no penguins in the Arctic, only the Antarctic 5. You have made $300 in profit 6. You would ask, "What door would the other guard tell me to use?" (Then you would go through the door you were told not to use.) 7. The Z goes above the line since the letters above the line are made up of straight lines and those below the line are made up of curved lines. 8. Heather and Daisy grow ivy and violets. Lily and Violet grow heather and roses. Rose and Ivy grow lilies and daisies.

UNIT 3 JUST FOR FUN pages 96–97

REMEMBERING WHAT YOU SEE

2 story house (page 96)	1 story house (page 97)
door in center	door at side
dog on lawn	cat in window
shrubbery	garden in front
curtains	window shades
bow windows	standard windows
smoking chimney	no chimney
deciduous trees	evergreen trees
mailbox at curb	mailbox by door
sedan at curb	station wagon in driveway
basketball hoop in driveway	no basketball hoop
no lights	lights flanking door
no fence	fence
clouds	no clouds
garage	no garage

UNIT 7 JUST FOR FUN page 223

WORD SEARCH

```
A X T F R O S M W R Z E L E C T R O N I C P O R R C
N E V I R T U A L R E T Z M F S U V I L U W F U I X
X Z F O T I P U Z R Y X N B K G M P C K B L O Z U L
P X E A R R E O O P K M Q L S R I R O J B P M K D S
O Q T P C A R T D J M E G A S I T E S F Y B O O K L
T I O E T X S O R T Z F J T O N U Q Z L H N G A E T
R K E T I K T R C A B R B T I T E C H N O L O G Y A
V S A O O F O U Q M O N L I N E Q R E X L T I O B U
B L I O R O R S T P F J G L O R E N T E E L B A O R
T P B R E A E P B F N Z S E T N L O M L X Y U R A Z
V E R A P H U Z I N T C P S N E M E P R E M T O R I
N J H F N I Z Q U J L A I E R T R E D I D Z A O D T
S H O P P I N G M A L L S F I I R I W F I R M S O E
L F I T Q P W N Z B I A O M N W R E I N Z Q I U Z M
F N A R K P R A N T B I F L E O Q N P I N R T B Y O
C W A S B L O R B A O R T E C O M M E R C E O T J Z
R E T A I L Z A T R M O W F L A C S H F E Z T I U T
B B F N Q J G A R Z P M A E I Q R F I Z Y N L F B L
R S A B D C D M L Y O Z R Y C E N B T O J U E O I L
A I F X I O N A V R C E E D K E L R L E G E B U S M
K T R B U A B Z E E S O L C D E O C O N S U M E R S
H E I Z L O R O D R T G A N E R P Y A L I A I N H R
Y A S U R F I N G M N H T C V J U R Z E Y C N P A Z
E N F T O I L K Y D R A O F Z A P O J E L T M W H I
```

UNIT 8 JUST FOR FUN page 260

WORD SCRAMBLE

1. cynical 2. creativity 3. genius 4. intelligence 5. enthusiasm 6. emotional 7. factor 8. theory 9. Einstein

Unit 1—Language and Life

1. Eva Hoffman, *Lost in Translation: A Life in a New Language* (New York: E. P. Dutton 1989), 146–147.
2. Shanti Menon, "The Bilingual Brain," *Discover* (October, 1997): 26. © 1997. Reprinted with permission of *Discover Magazine*.
3. Richard Lederer, *The Play of Words* (New York: Pocket Books, 1990), 181, 183.
4. Alan Benjamin, *A Treasury of Baby Names* (New York: Signet Books, 1991), 215–218.
5. Ian Baker, "Friendship." Reprinted by permission.

Unit 2—Polar Connection

1. Sharon McAuliffe, "Strange Wonders in a Strange Land," *Omni*, 1, no. 4 (January, 1995): 56.
2. John Koch, "Interview with Heather Urquhart," *Boston Globe Magazine*, (February 25, 1996): 12.
3. From: "FIRE AND ICE" *from* THE POETRY OF ROBERT FROST edited by EDWARD CONNERY LATHEM, Copyright 1951 by Robert Frost, Copyright 1923, © 1969 by Henry Holt and Company. Reprinted by permission of Henry Holt and Company, Inc.
4. Laura Tangley, "Cracks in the Arctic Ice: News of a Great Big Melt in Earth's Past," *U.S. News and World Report* (July 13, 1998): 52. Copyright, July 13, 1998, **U.S. News and World Report.**
5. Andrew Purvis, "Go with the Floe," *Time*, (August 3, 1998).
6. McAuliffe, "Strange Wonders in a Strange Land," 56.
7. Wallace Broeker, quoted in Eugene Linden, "Warnings from the Ice," *Time* (April 14, 1997): 54.
8. Corey S. Powell, with reporting by Nurit Bloom, *Discover* (May 1998).

Unit 3—There's No Place Like Home

1. Daniel Fost, "Asian Homebuyers Seek Wind and Water," *American Demographics* 15, no. 6 (June 1993): 23; Evelyn Lip, "Feng Shui for the Home" (Torrance, California: Heian International, 1996); Carol Wolf, "Searching for Good Chi: Feng Shui Ideas Offer Business Greater Energy," *Crain's Cleveland Business* 14, no. 50 (December 13, 1993): 15.
2. Daniel Lourie, "My House." Reprinted by permission.
3. Andy Warhol, *From A to B and Back Again* (1975).
4. John Berger, *Harper's* (January 1987).
5. Spoken by the character Fran Eva in Herman Hesse, *Demian* (1960).
6. Primo Levi, "My House," *Other People's Trades* (1985).

Unit 4—Athletes and Role Models

1. "Superlatives," *The Economist* 347, no. 80/1 (June 6, 1998): 59. © Copyright 1998 The Economist Newspaper Group, Inc. Reprinted with permission. Further reproduction prohibited.
2. Quoted in "Show Me the Money: Do Pro Athletes Make Too Much Money?" *Current Events* 96, no. 26 (May 5, 1997): 1.
3. George Orwell, *Shooting an Elephant.*
4. Hayward Hale Broun, quoted in James Michener, *Sports in America.*

Unit 5—Your Place in the Family

1. Judith Viorst, *Necessary Losses* (1986).
2. Ellen Galinsky, *Between Generations* (1981).
3. Jane Nelson, *Positive Discipline* (1981).

Unit 6—Influential Entertainers

1. Quoted in *Screen International* [London], May 1976.
2. Quoted in *Halliwell's Filmgoer's Companion* (1984).

Unit 7—Entrepreneurs in the Electronic Age

1. Kelly J. Andrews, online editor, "Amazon.com Builds a Web Retail Business by the Book," *Entrepreneurial Edge* 2 (Spring, 1997).
2. Andrews, "Amazon.com," Spring, 1997.
3. Michael Meyer, "Going Shopping.com," *Newsweek* (August 17, 1998): 45.
4. "Jeff Bezos," *Chain Store Age* 73, no. 9 (September 1997): 70.
5. Andrews, "Amazon.com," Spring, 1997.
6. Andrews, "Amazon.com," Spring, 1997.
7. Aaron Zitner, "Cybermedicine Seen as Unhealthy by Some," *Boston Globe,* 6 August, 1998, pp. C1, C5. Reprinted courtesy of *The Boston Globe.*

Unit 8—IQ or EQ

1. Edgard Varese, quoted by Martha Graham, *The New York Times,* 31 March 1985.
2. "They Burn So Bright," *Newsweek* (June 28, 1993): 51–53. From Newsweek, June 28, © 1993, Newsweek, Inc. All rights reserved. Reprinted by permission.
3. Dean Keith Simonton, quoted in Sharon Begley, "The Puzzle of Genius," *Newsweek* (June 23, 1993): 50.
4. Howard Gardner, quoted in Begley, "The Puzzle of Genius," p. 48.
5. Patricia Hassler, review of *Emotional Intelligence,* Booklist 92, no. 2 (September 15, 1995): 11.
6. "The EQ Factor," *Time* (October 2, 1995): 66.
7. "The EQ Factor," *Time*, p. 66.
8. Alfred North Whitehead, Dialogues.

TEXT CREDITS

Unit 1—Language and Life

"What Would You Like in Your Welcome Package? Immigrants Offer Tips for an Official Guide to America" by David W. Chen. Published in the *New York Times,* July 4, 1998. Copyright © 1998 by the New York Times Co. Reprinted by permission.

"A 'glorious mongrel'" by Gerald Parshall. Published in *U.S. News and World Report,* September 25, 1996. Copyright, September 25, 1996, **U.S. News & World Report.**

"My Name" by Sandra Cisneros. From THE HOUSE ON MANGO STREET. Copyright © 1984 by Sandra Cisneros. Published by Vintage Books, a division of Random House, Inc., and in hardcover by Alfred A. Knoph in 1994. Reprinted by permission of Susan Bergholz Literary Services, New York. All rights reserved.

Unit 2—Polar Connection

"Antarctica: A Lonely Planet Travel Survival Kit" by Jeff Rubin. Published by *Lonely Planet Publications,* Oakland, California, 1996. Reprinted with permission of Lonely Planet Publications.

"Survival of the Coldest," by Jeff Rubin. Published in Audubon, November–December 1996. Excerpted from the *Lonely Planet Guide to Antarctica* by Jeff Rubin. Published by *Lonely Planet Publications,* Oakland, California, 1996. Reprinted by permission of the author.

"Cool Science on Antarctica: Why Do Scientists Flock to the Coldest, Windiest Place on Earth?" by Chana Freiman Steifel. From SCIENCE WORLD, September 8, 1997. Copyright © 1997 by Scholastic Inc. Reprinted by permission of Scholastic Inc.

Unit 3—There's No Place Like Home

"Coming Home: Gay Talese." Published in *USAir Magazine*, August 1994.

"Coming Home: Richard Ford." Interview by Abigail Seymour. Published in *US Airways Magazine*, March 1997, 86. Published by Pace Communications. Reprinted by permission.

"Does Boston Mind Its Manners?" by Scott Lehigh. Published in the *Boston Globe*, December 16, 1996. Reprinted courtesy of The Boston Globe.

"The House on Mango Street" by Sandra Cisneros. From THE HOUSE ON MANGO STREET. Copyright © 1984 by Sandra Cisneros. Published by Vintage Books, a division of Random House, Inc., and in hardcover by Alfred A. Knoph in 1994. Reprinted by permission of Susan Bergholz Literary Services, New York. All rights reserved.

Unit 4—Athletes and Role Models

"Athletes and Role Models" by Sheila Globus. Published in *Current Health*, February 1998. Reprint permission granted, *Current Health 2®*, copyright © 1998, published by Weekly Reader Corporation. Further reproduction is prohibited without permission from Weekly Reader Corporation. All rights reserved.

"I'm Not a Role Model" by David Gelman with Karen Springen and Sudarsan Raghavan. Published in *Newsweek*, June 28, 1993. From Newsweek, June 28, © 1993, Newsweek, Inc. All rights reserved. Reprinted by permission.

"Warning: Games Seriously Damage Health: Olympic Athletes Are Doubtful Role Models for Average Citizen." Editorial. Published in *The Lancet,* August 3, 1996. © Copyright by The Lancet Ltd. 1996.

Unit 5—Your Place in the Family

"Rebels Among Us: Birth Order and Personality" by Karen Lindell. Published in *LA Parent*, 1997. Reprinted by permission.

"A Telling Birthmark for Businesses: Researcher Says How C.E.O.'s Act Is Linked to Order in the Family" by Judith H. Dobrzynski. Published in the *New York Times*, February 21, 1997. Copyright © 1997 by the New York Times Co. Reprinted by permission.

"The Stones" from *You Can't Have Everything*, by Richard Shelton, © 1975. Reprinted by permission of the University of Pittsburgh Press.

Unit 6—Influential Entertainers

"The TV Host: Oprah Winfrey" by Deborah Tannen. *Time Magazine*, June 8, 1998. © Copyright Deborah Tannen. Reprinted by permission.

"The TV Star: Lucille Ball" by Richard Zoglin. Published in *Time*, June 8, 1998. © Copyright Time Inc. Reprinted by permission.

"The TV Creator: Jim Henson" by James Collins. Published in *Time*, June 8, 1998. © Copyright Time Inc. Reprinted by permission.

Unit 7—Entrepreneurs in the Electronic Age

"The Virtual Route to Happiness" by Ann Treneman. Published in *The Independent Tabloid*, [London] October 9, 1997. Reprinted by permission.

"Click Till You Drop" by Michael Frantz. Published in *Time*, July 20, 1998. © Copyright Time Inc. Reprinted by permission.

Unit 8—IQ or EQ

"The Art of Genius: Eight Ways to Think Like Einstein" by Michael Michalko. Published in *Utne Reader*, July–August 1998. Originally appeared in the May 1998 issue of THE FUTURIST. Used with permission from the World Future Society, 7910 Woodmont Avenue, Suite 450, Bethesda, Maryland 20814. 301/656-8274; Fax 301/951-0394; http://www.wfs.org/wfs.

"The E-Factor!" by Mary C. Hickey. Published in *Ladies' Home Journal*, September 1995. © Copyright 1995, Meredith Corporation. All rights reserved. Used with permission of *Ladies' Home Journal*.

"The Lowdown on High EQ" by Timothy Dumas. Published in *Cosmopolitan*, January 1996, 162–166. Reprinted courtesy *Cosmopolitan Magazine*, Hearst Corporation.